TRUST:
The CEO's Currency for Success

The ASSET
that doesn't show on the balance sheet

FRANK WAPOLE

ISBN-10: 146649848X
ISBN-13: 9781466498488

Dedication

To my wife Pat, my family, and friends who encouraged me to put my beliefs of leadership into this narrative. My hope is that the leadership philosophy of *Trust: The CEO's Currency for Success* resonates with the leaders who are in a position to bring positive change to our public and private institutions' environments.

Acknowledgements

Everyone I spoke to about this project shaped the material through their candid observations.

For their time and input, I thank Chris Banakis, Ben Belmonte, Dick Day, Karen Gilligan, Phil Grinstead, Eileen Herdrich, Herb Johnson, Ed McLoughlin, Janet Pucino, Ed Rys, Bernie Schaeffer, Michaele Skowron, Dennis Strand, Bruce Swail, Brian Wapole, Eric Wapole, Rod Wapole, Lawre Weiner, and Dave Williams.

A special thank you to these folks who walked with me from the first version of every chapter until it evolved into a coherent body of thought: Tom Berger, Wendy Diamond, Bob Girard, Jim Haleem, Ginny Hanson, Gabriele Hilberg, Art Seymour, and Colleen Wapole.

My deepest appreciation to Glen Phillips for his direction on book structure; to Andre Echevarria and Robin Katz for their creativity on the graphics, and to Mary Jane Grinstead for her energy and skill in organizing the flow of the book for the benefit of the material and of the reader.

Contents

Section 1

Is Your End of the Boat Sinking, or Is It Just Mine?

Across all parts of society, people are uncertain and anxious about the future of business, government, and even our way of life.

In all of our institutions—public and private, profit and nonprofit—there have been failures. Institutions have died off prematurely. We have seen whole industries and global capital markets seize up and implode, resulting in jobs being lost forever.

Our free enterprise system has been shaken to its roots. All of us are affected by our institutions failing to live up to their full long-term potential. Our success at maintaining and creating jobs in the private sector long-term is at the core of our existence as a nation. Personal finances, institutional assets, and government tax receipts all depend on jobs.

It has taken the narrow, short-term focus of multiple generations of leadership in public and private, profit and non-profit institutions to put us in such a precarious economic position.

The actions that have been taken to plug the holes in our ship and bail us out have fallen short resulting in further eroding our country's way of life and our trust in our leaders.

We are running out of financial resources while missing the framing to be able to learn from our experiences to implement solutions to correct our course.

What caused the hole in the boat?

For decades, we as a society and as individuals have been so committed to individual and special interests that we have been willing to compromise, and in many cases, sell out the long-term sustainability of our institutions to satisfy short-term goals.

In business and in government, leaders and participants have deflected accountability for long-term goals. Protections and oversight have been ineffective in either blocking or changing people's behavior.

As awareness of the complexity and intricacies of the problems we face has skyrocketed, we have become less and less confident of a path out.

Trust in our leaders has plummeted. Trust comes from multiple events of being and feeling included; distrust can take root from one event of being and feeling excluded. Without a larger, longer time frame in which participants can see that their expectations are being at least considered, trust erodes and eventually is destroyed.

If participants do not trust their leaders, no matter what is being said even if it is factual, they are not going to believe them and, therefore, are not going to support them. When enough participants lose trust, institutions fail. And when institutions fail, societies, cultures, economies, and whole countries fail. Recorded history is replete with examples. Will the United States become another?

Our boat doesn't have to sink

If the leaders of this country's institutions are willing, we can work our way out of this morass.

Trust: The CEO's Currency for Success supplies the philosophical starting point, a pragmatic methodology, and tools for change. This is based on an expanded frame that considers the long-term impact of every short-term decision.

When applied, this model:

- Resets the hyper-focus from individual, short-term objectives to job retention and job growth through long-term institutional sustainability as measured by the P&L and balance sheet,

- Requires leaders and participants to deliver on their stated commitments and responsibilities,

- Produces an environment where all participants can trust that they are included in their leaders' vision and frame, and

- Helps participants give up the cynicism and impatience that keeps them from recognizing and acknowledging any good in their leaders' actions.

Until leaders can express their vision in a broader frame, trust will continue to be lost and not rebuilt. Leaders who are serious about regaining the trust of their participants will start by demonstrating passion and commitment to their long-term responsibility to the business institution.

In return, participants must then see and be willing to acknowledge that their leaders are considering the desires and expectations of *all* the business's participants through their priority setting and decision making.

Working together in this way, CEOs and participants will rebuild trust—the asset that doesn't appear on the balance sheet. Implementing this model of inclusiveness and diversity of thought will right this ship.

The audience for this material is both current and future leaders of all institutions.

- Current leaders in both the public and private sectors who see the need for leadership behavior change and are willing to role model that change

- Influencers of those leaders: Boards of directors, voters, union leaders, think tanks, and thought leaders

- Future leaders and influencers of future leaders: students, parents, teachers, college and university professors, and participants in MBA and other graduate leadership programs

Although leaders in *all* institutions need to recalibrate how they view their roles and responsibilities, our business and government leaders must lead the charge. They control the resources and regulations that determine our economies through the behaviors of the people who participate.

The material in this book is presented in three sections:

- Section 1: Analyzes the beliefs and behaviors that created our current economic environment.

- Section 2: Introduces two new tools, RoundTable and BusinessLoop, which the leaders of all institutions can use to reverse the behaviors that are causing job loss and institutional failure.

- Section 3: Presents a methodology for CEOs and other leaders to apply these tools.

Trust: The CEO's Currency for Success reflects my experience in public and privately held business institutions. However, this philosophy of leadership and the tools that support it are applicable for all leaders of all institutions.

Chapter 1

A New, More Inclusive Frame

Tigers inside the gates

*T*here is a folk story about a once prosperous, self-contained village that lay at the very edge of a large jungle. The villagers worked hard for their livelihood and raised their families to do the same. They cautioned their children to live and think independently while being responsible citizens of the community.

The early villagers had long ago erected a tall, strong fence between the jungle and the village. The fence had a gate that was locked and always guarded. The villagers trusted that the fence would protect them. On occasion, the village elders would open the gate and venture into the jungle. They would return in silence with frowns, secure the gate, and direct the guards to keep it locked for the good of the village. The village was self-sufficient, so the villagers didn't concern themselves about what went on beyond the fence.

One day two of the villagers came to wonder if there might be something outside the fence that would make life better and easier for them and their businesses. Determined to see and sample what was beyond, these two men went around the guards and quietly slipped through the gate.

They expected that the jungle would be dense and hard to penetrate, but it gave way without effort. They soon came upon a broad, sunny clearing *with piles of food, golden objects, and embroidered silk clothing. They were so engaged by this wondrous sight that they were taken by complete surprise when a beautiful, fearsome tiger appeared and began to speak.*

"All this can be yours," said the tiger as he swept his giant, long-clawed paw over the vast treasures. "This jungle holds no dangers that the village needs to guard against. These rewards are waiting for those who are willing to take them. Just leave the gate open so it will be easier for you to return and take more."

The men gathered up all they could hold and carried their newfound inventory back into the village through the unlocked gate. The tiger and his many friends quietly followed.

The gate is open and the tigers are among us

Whether we or someone else made the decision to open the gate and let the tigers in, we are all affected.

Much has been written and discussed about the shrinking of the globe. We may have been successful in the past in a perceived global environment of fenced in societies, institutions, and humans interacting as unconnected entities and individuals.

More than ever, I agree with those writers, philosophers, thinkers, mystics, government people, and businesspeople who recognize the interconnectivity of all of us in all of our institutions through all of our behaviors. Seen or unseen, everything and everyone has an influence on everything and everyone else.

Now might be one of the few times in history when most of us, if not everyone, will feel and be affected by this inner-connectivity. Just as a fence cannot guard against tigers forever or keep people from making poor decisions, limiting the frame to the current perceived environment does not negate the reality that always exists beyond. The reality was that tigers were always in the villagers' frame, but the villagers didn't recognize it until they opened the gate.

Whatever frame the CEO is presently holding to understand all the influences on the business institution, no frame can account for all the possible influences and connections that exist. It might be difficult or impossible to deal with all the pieces, but such is our collective reality.

Frame has different meanings to different people. To the cosmologist, it is the universe. To a photographer, it is the moment in time that the camera records after adjusting for distance and light. To a business person, it is the activities and influences taken into consideration that will affect the business plan now and into the future (customers, competitors, pricing, regulations, and so on).

Cosmologists believe that everything has an influence on everything else. Yet even with floors and floors of Cray computers, they have not been able to model all the hidden influences of pure energy and physical matter in the universe. Even the brightest minds with the best computers cannot act with certainty given the complexity of these relationships. Cosmologists accept this reality and make the best judgments possible always with the recognition that there are unseen influences beyond their understanding.

The same idea applies to CEOs. Imagine the influences and relationships that exist among all the 6.8 billion people on planet Earth—both one on one and through institutions. Among these, certainly, are influences that CEOs cannot or do not see. In addition, all influences have linkages that go in many directions. For any one company, these linkages may be unique, but they do always exist and are never fully known.

However, all this complexity does not remove the need to make decisions. Like the cosmologist, the CEO must make decisions to go forward and prepare as best he can for the surprises that will come.

It is fairly straightforward to say that unlike cosmologists, CEOs can disregard the influence of Saturn on their business frames. They cannot afford to disregard the influence of the next institution or the next set of people, especially over time, even if these influences, like Saturn, are beyond their frame and control.

If we could see or even imagine what all the possible influences and changes could be over time, we might believe we could imagine the perfect solution, but we can't. It is more important to make sure that the question being asked is reflective of the issue that we are trying to address. So before we can get to the answer, we ask what is happening that's generating the question. Who is affected and how are they affected? Along with observing the issue's influence correctly, what is the prioritization of solving it compared to other issues and opportunities? This is what I mean by a larger frame—decision making based on understanding and prioritizing the issue/opportunity before discussing possible actions.

When we use a larger frame based on beliefs that are true to make decisions, participants are better able to accept an answer because they trust the process by which it was derived and the integrity of the person delivering it—not because it is deemed the "perfect" answer. There is no perfect answer that will hold forever. The important words are "larger frame" and "over time."

Reframing the relationships between the institution, the CEO, and the human participants

This methodology begins with the reframing of the relationship between the institution, participants, and their leaders. In this new framing the institution is a separate entity requiring life management.

INSTITUTION

The institution is acknowledged as a separate and distinct entity. The goal of the institution is to live an acceptable quality of life for as long as it satisfies its owners and participants.

The human life span—long or short—is determined by our personal DNA, the environment, and the choices that we make. Just as humans have a life span, so do institutions.

This comparison underscores the inherent uniqueness of each entity and suggests that an institution's DNA, like human DNA, sets a framework for its longevity and quality of life. Internal and external events, decisions, and the environment will maximize or minimize this longevity and quality of life given the institution's DNA and how well it satisfies its human participants' ongoing expectations.

Long-term sustainability is not immortality or forever; it is defined by the desires and support of the institution's owners, whether the institution is publically or privately held. An institution's quality and span of life (sustainability) is determined by its unique DNA and the degree to which it satisfies the appropriate expectations of all participants (the owners, employees, suppliers, and customers) through the vision and behavior of the CEO.

We readily see the need for a human life to be managed and protected so that it has a chance to achieve its fullest potential, but we haven't demonstrated the same concern for our government and business institutions. Just as we are recognizing in a more complete way that human behavior affects other life forms and ecosystems around the globe, so also do our personal behavior and choices affect the long-term sustainability of our institutions.

An institution needs a lot of help to be born and to evolve through its formative years. It needs care, feeding, and nurturing to survive. However, unlike a human, an institution can never reach the state where it is self-sustaining. While participants can make choices and speak for themselves, the institution can never make its own decisions and has no voice of its own. The business institution requires someone to think and make decisions unemotionally for it. That someone is the CEO.

The role of the CEO is different from every other role in the institution

CEOs are unique men and women who have the mental capacity matched by a strong sense of responsibility to the institution, its owners, its employees, its customers, and all the other groups involved.

Leadership is responsible for the institution's long-term sustainability compatible with the institution's DNA and the desires of all the participants.

LEADERSHIP

Whether in government or business, when the convergence of events gives an individual the opportunity to become CEO, that person owns responsibility for the long-term sustainability of the institution. It is his first priority.

Without the institution, the CEO doesn't exist. Without the CEO's vision, guidance, expression, and protection, the institution cannot perform to its fullest potential. This symbiotic relationship between the CEO and the institution gives the best odds for the most people to have their lives positively affected.

CEOs must demonstrate through their words and behavior that they hold a broad enough frame to consider the disparate expectations and commitments of all those participating. They must act with integrity and with the long-term sustainability of the institution as their guiding principle. They must guard against being misguided by the inappropriate emphasis on demands of special interests or their own short-term incentives as they make and cause others to make decisions.

When he or she accepts the job, the CEO becomes the mind and the voice of the institution. We want the mind of the CEO to be unemotional when thinking and making decisions for the institution. We want the voice of the CEO to be passionate and charismatic when connecting as a human being with participants as he or she shares decisions.

When CEOs do not represent the business institution in this manner they are not doing the job. And if they aren't doing it, who can? The answer, as we are all too painfully aware, is no one.

All people involved with or affected by the institution are viewed by the separate entity as participants

With the institution being a separate entity and the CEO being its mind and voice to carry out the goal of long-term sustainability, a redefinition of the people participating to achieve this goal is required.

PARTICIPANTS

The people who participate in the institution earn their wants, needs, and expectations by delivering on their committed contributions over time.

To the institution, all people are participants regardless of the subgroup that they are in. Assuming an institution has more than one employee and at least some customers, participants include community, government, investors, owners, board of directors, employees, customers, suppliers, and partners.

Each subgroup has its own special interests and expectations of the institution that are financial and human in nature and expressed or unexpressed. From the institution's perspective, special interests do not equal special treatment. The CEO is aware of these different interests and how they vary from one to the next.

While the institution does not hold any one expectation or desire as more special than another, the owners of the institution do receive a higher coefficient of interest from the CEO. It is the CEO's responsibility to create an environment for making decisions that balance the financial health of the institution and to deliver on the expectations of all the participants, while holding them responsible for delivering on their agreed-to contributions.

Participants—along with wanting their needs, desires, and expectations ("gets")—must be committed to delivering their agreed-upon contributions ("gives"). Even though some individuals' "gets" may be short-term focused, all participants must recognize how their "gives" contribute to the long-term sustainability of the institution, which won't necessarily be maximum short-term profits or immortality.

If all or most of the participants are in agreement not to deliver on their commitments, and if the institution cannot survive without their commitments, then the institution will, or should, go out of existence.

The CEO balances the relationships between the institution and all participants

The frame of reality considers a long-term measurement in which all participants (including the CEO) tend to be short-term relative to the institution being long-term. Further, the CEO's role is not complete until he or she hands the company off to the next CEO who is willing to take on the number-one priority of long-term sustainability for the institution.

To earn the trust of all participants whose needs cannot be met in the short-term (however short-term is defined), the CEO must demonstrate by both words and actions that he or she is holding a long-term frame for the sustainability of the business institution that *does* consider the needs and expectations of all participants.

The institution is indifferent to what is happening as long as there is balance with the participants and they are satisfied with their relationship with the institution. This is at the foundation of rebuilding trust in all the participant relationships. We want all the participants, not just a few, to feel they are considered in the CEO's beliefs as well as her behavior.

In this new framing, no matter the size of the business, its stage of growth, its current performance, or whether it is privately or publically held, CEOs achieve the company's long-term sustainability through managing and balancing the shorter-term desires and commitments of all the participants to the CEO's vision for the longer-term. Figure 1.1 illustrates the balanced relationships that produce an environment of trust. Trust is the asset that doesn't show on the balance sheet.

Every CEO must navigate and balance the differences in the expectations and commitments of the participants with the complexity of their interrelationships. In this environment every short-term decision is made in consideration of its effect on the long-term sustainability of the business institution.

Figure 1.1: Relationships in Balance Produce Trust

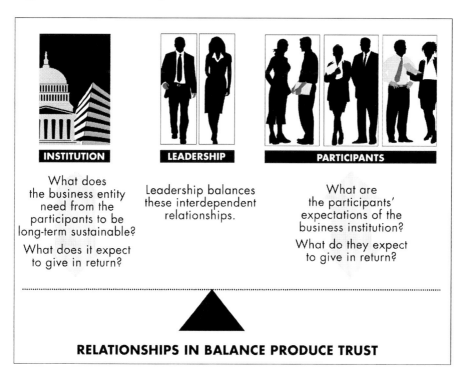

INSTITUTION

What does the business entity need from the participants to be long-term sustainable?

What does it expect to give in return?

LEADERSHIP

Leadership balances these interdependent relationships.

PARTICIPANTS

What are the participants' expectations of the business institution?

What do they expect to give in return?

RELATIONSHIPS IN BALANCE PRODUCE TRUST

Out-of-balance relationships produced the current environment of the benefits to few

We and the people that we depend on to get the job done—employees, customers, suppliers, regulators, board members, investors, and others—are steeped in a culture of special interests. Each interest wants and believes it should have its expectations met in the short-term regardless of the consequences to the rest or the participants or the long-term sustainability of the institution.

Priorities are set and decisions are made within a too-small frame of reality that inappropriately validates the influence of some interests. This prioritization almost always benefits a few—usually the CEO along with a limited set of participants—at the expense of the business institution and the remainder of the participants.

CEOs of publicly traded companies are under incredible pressure from inappropriate demands of Wall Street, boards of directors, and investors for short-term financial returns. Additionally, CEO compensation that is entirely focused on short-term measurements, earnings per share, and stock price has virtually guaranteed the failure of CEOs and other leaders to carry out their responsibility to the long-term sustainability of our business institutions.

This out of balance environment (Figure 1.2) tests even the most forward-thinking CEO who wants to hand over to a successor a constantly rejuvenating institution that has a healthy future beyond the current CEO's desire to lead it.

Figure 1.2: Relationships Out of Balance Produce Benefits to Few

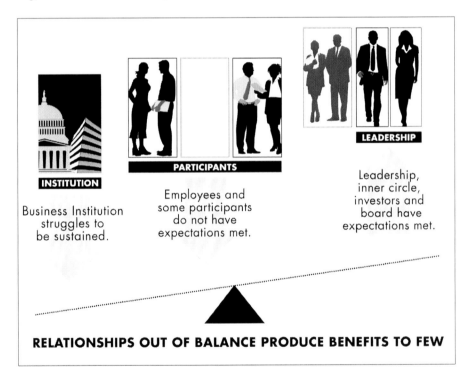

INSTITUTION
Business Institution struggles to be sustained.

PARTICIPANTS
Employees and some participants do not have expectations met.

LEADERSHIP
Leadership, inner circle, investors and board have expectations met.

RELATIONSHIPS OUT OF BALANCE PRODUCE BENEFITS TO FEW

Over the last two-plus decades, these behaviors have produced the savings and loan crisis, the burst of the dot-com bubble, the destruction of the real estate market, and the near-collapse of the financial markets and banking industry.

Some participants are getting an unequal gain from their involvement and contributions. Special interests, personal short-term goals, and financial incentives trump long-term sustainability with leaders and participants deflecting accountability, while government protections and oversight have been ineffective.

Think about your own environment. Do you consider all participants when you are making a decision, or do you fall into the trap of thinking about only a subset of them?

Changing the current environment from the *benefit to few* to the desired environment of trust

Figure 1.3 compares how the CEO and the participants believe and behave in an environment of trust compared to an environment that benefits few.

Figure 1.3: Contrasting thoughts, beliefs, and business behaviors of the current and desired environments

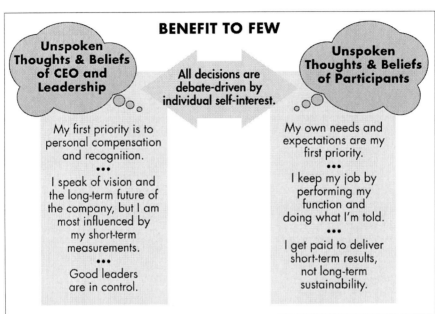

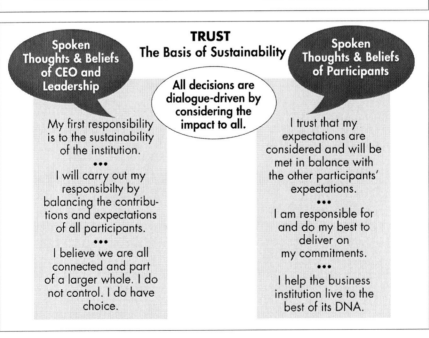

The environment that benefits few is led by an "all-knowing" CEO. The CEO's and participants' thoughts and beliefs are not visible and open. Behaviors are driven by self-interest and self-protection.

In the trust environment, led by an open and inclusive CEO, the thoughts and beliefs of the CEO and participants are open and shared along with the goal of long-term sustainability. Participants recognize the impact of their behavior on the institution as a whole as they prioritize and make decisions.

The CEO's challenge is to move from the special-interests environment that benefits few to an environment that promotes trust

The scope and complexity of the problems that CEOs and business owners face as the architects of transformation cannot be overstated. However, the process of finding a solution begins with us as leaders addressing our individual behavior in this current environment of special interests. We must have the courage and confidence to rise above the pressure for short-term financial performance and have our behavior balance short-term survival with the long-term sustainability of our business institutions.

To change the environment we must change old behaviors to new behaviors. To change behaviors we must change the ingrained beliefs behind those behaviors. We must first understand our existing beliefs about leadership and how they produced the current environment of limited frame for priority setting and decision making.

The material in this book will challenge you to reassess and possibly change your behavior as the leader of your institution. To begin, let's establish a baseline of your leadership behaviors. Mark where you feel you are on each of the continuums in CEO Exercise 1.

CEO Exercise 1: My Current Business Behaviors

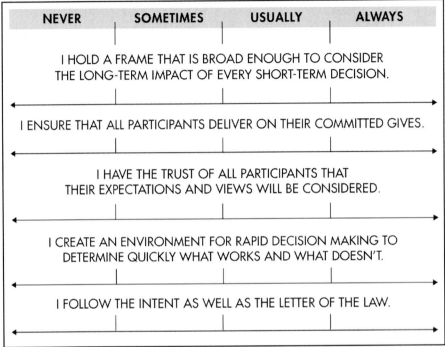

NEVER	SOMETIMES	USUALLY	ALWAYS

I HOLD A FRAME THAT IS BROAD ENOUGH TO CONSIDER
THE LONG-TERM IMPACT OF EVERY SHORT-TERM DECISION.

I ENSURE THAT ALL PARTICIPANTS DELIVER ON THEIR COMMITTED GIVES.

I HAVE THE TRUST OF ALL PARTICIPANTS THAT
THEIR EXPECTATIONS AND VIEWS WILL BE CONSIDERED.

I CREATE AN ENVIRONMENT FOR RAPID DECISION MAKING TO
DETERMINE QUICKLY WHAT WORKS AND WHAT DOESN'T.

I FOLLOW THE INTENT AS WELL AS THE LETTER OF THE LAW.

Assuming you didn't place all of your marks beneath "ALWAYS," under what conditions do you feel it is acceptable not to? You will be comparing this assessment of your current behavior with how you will want to operate once you have been exposed to the new beliefs and tools of trust.

In Chapter 2, we talk about how to realign leaders' beliefs and behaviors to rebuild an environment of trust.

Chapter 2

CEO Beliefs Drive CEO Behavior

"The worst derangement of the spirit is to believe things because we want them to be so…not because we have seen them for what they are."

— Jacques Bossuet, French theologian

CEO beliefs drive CEO behavior

As human beings, our beliefs are the stories that drive our behaviors. As CEOs, our personal and business beliefs shape everything we do and say. Regardless of our words or intent, all behavior is consciously or unconsciously driven by beliefs. Beliefs form the bedrock of who we are as leaders in business and as individuals in our personal lives.

But, as we all know, over time and with new information and perspective, beliefs can change.

That's because there are very few absolute truths for the human race and the physical universe, even if we make decisions and choices all our lives as if there were many more. Consider these old beliefs that we once held as true but, over time, found to be false and now no longer hold as true.

In science and medicine:

- The earth is the center of the universe.

- The sun is the center of the universe.

- The earth is flat.

- Smoking doesn't hurt you if you don't inhale.

- A doctor wouldn't prescribe a medication if it had negative side effects.

In business:

- Automobiles will never replace the horse.

- "Made in Japan" equals poor quality.

- The U.S. banking industry will never fail.

- Your home is the best investment you will ever make.

- The SEC will protect investors against fraud.

- What's good for General Motors is good for the country.

- Successful businesses will go on forever.

In politics:

- A Catholic can never be elected president of the United States.

- A woman can never be secretary of state.

- The United States will never elect an African-American president.

Now consider these current—but false—beliefs in business leadership.

- Short-term financial performance takes care of long-term sustainability.

- A good CEO delivers on the short-term measurements, no matter what.

- Shrewd CEOs don't let regulations and laws get in the way. They find the loopholes.

- A strong CEO makes the big decisions.

And the most limiting false beliefs of all:

- A good CEO can see it all.

- A good CEO has control.

If we can change our beliefs about all these other things, we can certainly change our beliefs about leadership, if we so choose. That is a choice we must make if we are going to fix the problems that are destroying the economy of this country from the inside out.

What do we believe today that we will find false tomorrow?

CEO Moments

As individuals we have all had those unexpected instances when we suddenly came to see an ordinary statement, activity, or responsibility in an entirely different way. A trigger—an event, an idea, or even a stranger's casual comment or question—causes us to view something familiar that we though we understood with a whole new awareness. These moments can clarify beliefs we already hold, or they can make us realize that we believe something that isn't true. Either way, they jar us, kind of like stepping on a rake. And once one of those events happens, the awareness doesn't go away.

My first CEO moment happened shortly after I began a European assignment as the Cold War was ending and the Iron Curtain was coming down. These political events were unexpected, like so many other experiences that came to be around this assignment.

During one of my early meetings in Germany, a European executive asked what my vision for our company in Europe was.

"Well, that's obvious, isn't it?" I thought. "It is to make the numbers and to deliver on my P&L responsibility." But then I hesitated, caught by that word "vision."

I realized in that moment that I didn't really have *my own* vision for the European operations. Along with taking on others' beliefs of leadership without questioning, I also picked up and accepted as my own the vision that was given to me by the U.S.-based corporation.

That vision didn't go beyond carrying out the operational activities of pursuing product and market segments, rationalizing the redundancy of assets and people by integrating the acquired company into Motorola, and setting up the resulting organization to run more efficiently while achieving its short-term financial goals.

In other words, my vision was making the numbers. It did not include a broader frame for longer-term thinking. It excluded influences I couldn't see. It assumed that someone from the United States had a better understanding of the European businesses than the Europeans who were responsible for in-country operations.

Under that limited U.S. vision (based on short-term goals), leaders and participants made many decisions without the long-term sustainability of the total business as the guiding principle.

I was at odds with the company's leadership when it came to such a short-term vision, but, worse, my own personal short-term goals and financial incentives had me at odds with myself. Although I firmly believed that longer-term sustainability should have been included in the corporation's vision for European operations, my personal behavior was out of synch with this core belief.

As that "rake" smacked me right in the forehead, I realized that I had committed to carrying out a vision that didn't match what I really felt and believed about my responsibility as a business leader. I recognized more clearly than I ever had before the connection between what a person believes and how a person behaves. I began to seriously question the drivers of the decisions I made and the hierarchy of their influences. What I believed about the CEO's ability to see and control all the influences that affect a company was different than the beliefs that the corporation's leadership was basing its vision on.

CEO MOMENT #1
To be truly powerful,
CEOs' stated visions must
be aligned with their
core beliefs.

CEO MOMENT

As I began challenging myself, I felt a growing conflict. I had been agreeing to behave as if a leader or team of leaders could see all the influences and have control over them, when at my core, I believed they couldn't.

As so often happens in life, when I was open and ready for a new way of viewing my world, a teacher appeared.

"Language, borders, cultures (LBC). This is what you will be dealing with."

That teacher was Herr Braxmeir, the retiring executive I was replacing.

I had been in Germany less than a week, when Herr Braxmeir invited me into his office. Straight-backed, he put a map of Europe on the wall and tapped it with the end of his gold pen. "I am going to give you one of the most valuable lessons of your life," he said in perfect but accented English.

Having grown up in Catholic schools, I was used to being lectured to, but this was my first experience in being taught by an old school, hierarchical and very formal German. I held still for it. What I learned from him that afternoon became the basis for the management philosophy and process that has worked for me ever since. His mapping of the business's participants, not his approach to leadership, is what impacted me.

"This map," Herr Braxmeir said, "shows the political boundaries of the countries in Europe as they are now." Then he took away the political boundaries and showed the same geography with the languages and dialects mapped in. How different these borders were! Then Herr Braxmeir layered in the cultures.

"Language, borders, cultures," he said. "This is what you will be dealing with."

Herr Braxmeir knew what he was talking about. In his own way, he was addressing my issue and adding specificity to my feeling of conflict between the belief that a CEO can see the whole and then control it and the reality that there is always a larger frame of reality than any CEO can ever see. And because of that, no person or group of people has the ability to control it all.

As I took on my new assignment I began to see with a new clarity how difficult it is for people coming from different perspectives and interests, holding different goals, and representing different constituencies to achieve the level of cooperation needed to solve a common problem or meet a common goal. I had plenty of experience with disconnects in a U.S. company—marketing and engineering, finance and sales, but never had I faced a challenge like this.

With executives from France, Germany, the United Kingdom, and the rest of the countries of Western Europe reporting to me, issues of communication through multiple languages weren't a surprise. As an English-only speaker in Germany, I was experiencing that all day long. Since meetings were conducted only in English, my European associates experienced the problem coming the other way.

Without Herr Braxmeir's tutorial, I would have made the assumption that if we somehow resolved the language issues we would be able to communicate. After his tutorial I was able to recognize that the challenge went much deeper.

The executives from the various countries would tell me about each other's stubbornness, but they couldn't see how their own beliefs and behaviors were contributing to our business problems. Or if they saw it, they weren't willing to acknowledge it in themselves and do what was necessary to overcome it. In this environment, trust certainly wasn't much of an asset on our balance sheet.

Each participant was constantly looking to behave in a way to gain or keep control. Each thought that he (and in that decade in Europe they were all male) knew everything there was to know about a particular issue. Not one of them trusted everyone else, and most of them trusted no one else. Their frame was their country's borders. There was no way that any of them wanted to make it easy for tigers from another country to get inside their gates.

The RoundTable mentality of inclusion and diversity of thought

After my LBC discussion with Herr Braxmeir, I began meetings by asking each person at the table to make his point in English. Then I would ask the next person to retell the point in English as they understood it. If there was a misunderstanding, it surfaced. We cleared it up, and then the person added his own point of view. Either he agreed with the view already given or explained why not and added a different perspective.

For the most part, the decisions we were discussing were mine to make. The participants eventually came to recognize that I was opening up the discussion to see the whole environment by including as much of their perspectives as possible before I made a decision.

But they were used to an autocratic and hierarchical method of making decisions. Even though it seemed to me they would prefer a more inclusive process that gave them the opportunity to express fully their concerns and points of view, I had to drag them into participating.

Eventually, they came to understand that this was the process I was going to follow and if they were going to influence me, it had to be at the table. Someone nicknamed our process RoundTabling, and the name stuck.

This RoundTable mentality, as I came to call it, did not allow for the backdoor diplomacy they were used to. I consistently demonstrated that I was going to drive decisions this way. There were situations where individuals withheld information. When that happened, I would bring everyone back to the table, reconvene the discussion, and we would have the new input shared openly with all.

As much as I wanted everyone to reconsider their old beliefs, buy in to this new way of leadership, and accept decisions made at the table, it didn't happen that way. The participants respected and followed the process, if for no other reason than that they all understood hierarchy, and I carried the title of "the boss." But as for them appreciating the process as a better way to manage and be managed, well, that was accepted to different levels and to different degrees. Becoming aware of their own beliefs and of the beliefs of others was enough to cause some of them to change. For the rest, awareness wasn't enough, and most stayed in their old beliefs that created their priorities and directed their behaviors.

I was the one who changed.

I gained a deeper understanding of the impact of a person's beliefs on the business institution. The same words do not communicate the same thing, whether in your first language, second, or third. As an American in Europe, through the powerful effect of language, borders, cultures, I started to see that people's personal and business beliefs are as influential and important to collaboration in business as job descriptions and tools are to the functional activities being coordinated. Armed with this new awareness, I created an environment for open and trusting communications with collaboration between people who didn't share a common language, came from different cultures, and were measured and paid in ways that drove them apart.

This environment produced better decisions, made more efficient use of resources, optimized operational and financial performance, and allowed for greater personal growth and satisfaction for the individuals involved. I came to realize that it was the way that business wanted to be run and would produce excellent results in any business environment.

I came to recognize my business beliefs because I was looking for better ways to solve a business problem.

My business beliefs:

- The CEO has a unique responsibility for the long-term sustainability of the business institution.

- Effective short-term decisions always consider the long-term impact.

- Relationships built on trust and respect are the basis for long-term sustainability.

- Diversity of all participants' perspectives leads to better decisions.

- The CEO is the integrity compass of the institution.

Once I recognized that my business beliefs were different from those around me and that my resulting business behavior produced better outcomes, it was hard to figure out why more leaders didn't see what I saw.

That's when I realized that my business beliefs came out of a deeper set of personal beliefs:

My Personal Beliefs:

- We are all connected.

- We cannot see the whole.

- No participant or institution lives forever.

And the most difficult to accept in our culture, I believe:

- No one person has control.

It takes a huge and healthy ego to be an effective CEO, so it might be very difficult to hold still for this. But a core truth of business and of life, whether we or our Boards, investors, or the financial community accept it, is that *we do not have control over anything.* No one, not even the most effective CEO in the world, can ever have control. What CEOs do have is their vision and their process for making choices and decisions in complex environments.

Speaking this truth does not mean that CEOs are not accountable or are shirking their responsibilities. It surely does not mean that they are not confident. CEOs actually must have supreme self-confidence and balance about who they are personally and as a leader to be able to say that they cannot control results by controlling others' behaviors.

Neither I nor any other CEO has total control of our environment. Not one of us can possibly see the whole of any situation or environment on our own. We cannot know all the details or the impacts on others. We might predict how others will react but we would not know for sure. We cannot control other's reactions, only our responses to their reactions.

CEO MOMENT #2
Although CEOs do not have control, they do have vision and choice.

CEO MOMENT

Once we begin to grasp the true meaning of what it is to be only a part of the whole and to have vision and choice but not control, we need a broader frame of relationships to see more of the whole of reality. The way to achieve that is through better coordination and collaboration of the business institution's participants. Believing and behaving any other way is actually detrimental to the viability of the companies we are leading.

CEO MOMENT #3
Collaboration, cooperation, and relationships built on trust and respect form the bridge from an environment that benefits few to the environment of trust.

CEO MOMENT

Your CEO Moments

CEO Moments appeared to me in a seemingly random fashion at first. Then I saw the hierarchy. I have had the time to reflect on my own experiences and awakenings and to lay out a more efficient process, which is the flow of this book.

The methodology within this book is based on new business beliefs that re-establish trust between all participants, especially trust in the CEO and in the institution as an intangible balance sheet asset.

It takes work to challenge the beliefs that we base our lives on, but demanding behavior change while not addressing those underlying beliefs is like choosing a diet to lose weight but not changing what we believe about food. We might achieve some short-term results, but if we are smart, we won't throw away our larger-sized clothes.

My European experience nudged me into my first CEO Moments and then jarred me to wake up and reflect upon my business beliefs about leadership. That forced me to re-examine my business behavior, which then caused me to consider underlying personal beliefs.

At the conclusion of each chapter are some of the questions that helped me gain a better understanding of my beliefs of leadership and their connection to my behavior. I encourage you to ask them of yourself to gain a better understanding of yours.

CEO REFLECTIONS

- Can you recognize how beliefs drive behavior?

- Do you believe you are always in control?

- Do you believe that you are ever in control?

- Do you ever feel like you have conflicting beliefs?

- Do you only assess others through their behavior or do you also try to understand their beliefs?

- Whom do you trust?

- Who trusts you?

- What percentage, if any, of the good will line on your balance sheet do you attribute to trust?

When you see your answers on paper, you will come up with some CEO Moments of your own. I recognized my CEO Moments, not because I was looking for them but because I was open.

- What will be the events that create CEO Moments for you?

- When CEO Moments arrive will you be ready and open to them?

- Has the rake already hit you and you haven't realized it until now?

Our business institutions need more corporate leaders who invite and encourage the discussion of current beliefs on leadership. But once we start examining our personal beliefs, talking about them, and telling people what they are, we are likely to learn something that causes us to see and accept that our beliefs have to change. This is frightening for most of us. That is why many business leaders make speeches, send out memos, and rely on company-wide programs in hopes of creating culture change without having to address the underlying beliefs that are creating the behavior and culture in the first place.

Section 2 supplies the new tools of RoundTable and Business-Loop for collaboration and coordination, bringing pragmatism to the philosophical statement of beliefs driving behavior.

My experiences and those of others demonstrate how enlightened CEOs can successfully apply these tools to the current business environment to create a new environment of informed, rapid, and efficient decision making based on trusting relationships. This approach leads to the long-term sustainability for the business institution while balancing the delivery of the expectations of all the participants.

In Section 3, we create a new frame for the CEO to move from the current to the desired environment by using the largest frame possible, the granularity of BusinessLoop, and the dialogue of RoundTable.

Section 2

New Tools for Trust

Two new management tools, RoundTable and BusinessLoop, manage the human relationships and the business activities between an institution and all internal and external participants. These tools came out of my European experience and evolved over my career. Why do we need new tools for business relationships and business activities? Because we are all feeling the impact of being connected while believing we are separate. The philosophical consideration of personal and business beliefs is transferred by pragmatic application of these new tools that align business behaviors.

Consider an example we are all too familiar with—the challenges of air travel. Airplanes are designed to fly, but they don't care where. Almost any mechanically-sound airplane can fly with a captain and crew. But to get a cabin full of passengers from Chicago to St. Louis safely requires the coordination of complex business activities through the relationships of humans, including ground personnel, FAA inspectors, and clear and well-maintained landing strips. The industry also needs tower systems, air traffic controllers, forecasts and warnings from weather experts, and extensive forethought and planning to ensure quick and correct responses when something does go wrong.

In arrival and departure cities, other businesses such as taxis, shuttles, hotels, airport restaurants, and ticketing kiosks are all part of the traveler's experience. Commuter traffic, equipment maintenance, union strikes, holidays, the price of oil, tornados in Oklahoma, icy runways in Chicago, or the threat of terrorism in London are just some of the many variables that can affect the way any single airplane flight delivers on the expectations of any single passenger.

Even with all the computers, electronics, and sophisticated robotic systems that are part of avionics, the responsibility for enabling planes to deliver passengers and cargo safely still falls to human participants with all their uniqueness and variability. It is the same for every business institution and for every CEO. It is impossible for any CEO or process to ever isolate entirely the business institution from the constant variability of other institutions and human behavior.

Our first priority when we fly is for the plane to arrive safely. We expect the airlines and the FAA to collaborate and coordinate—to be 100-percent successful in fulfilling this priority for us. We trust that they will do it. If we don't trust them, we won't fly. Airline companies put their money, people, and Six Sigma focus into getting the planes safely up and down, and it works. There are very few plane crashes. The other participants understand and support this as the number-one priority. You aren't going to ever hear the operator of a limo company say, "I wish they took a chance and took off in bad weather so our cars wouldn't have to wait for delayed flights."

Once the airlines handle safety, the rest of the travel experience is in the interfaces. That experience and those interfaces extend beyond row nine on a 757 to parking lots, rental car agencies, and the Internet. The airlines recognize that customers consider many more variables in assessing their travel experience beyond the actual flight. The airlines put ticket counters and skycaps outside at the curb and make online ticket ordering as simple as possible. They link up with business partners that perform other customer-related activities. Although the airlines cannot directly control another business's personnel, they can influence those people's behavior through their own employees' behavior and processes.

In some respects, a business institution is like a plane, an unemotional entity. The business exists to serve the needs and wants of participants just as airplanes exist to serve the needs of passengers. Vehicles can't do anything on their own; they depend on a complex network of human participants to give them life and value. Similarly, to give value back, the business requires the CEO for vision and voice, and it requires the participants to deliver on their commitments based on the priorities set by the CEO for the long-term sustainability of the institution.

The *human problems* in any business institution occur in the relationships between participants, whether those participants are internal or external. The RoundTable tool focuses on the *participants' issues*. The RoundTable methodology defines a repeatable and predictable way to create an environment where diverse participants can make their views known and then collaborate and coordinate on decisions made for the health of the P&L and balance sheet while supporting the priorities set by the CEO.

The CEO wants collaboration of people to take place at every human interface between the business functions but cannot be physically there at each activity and interface to make sure that this occurs.

The **RoundTable** tool addresses the human variability in relationships through collaboration.

ROUNDTABLE
For Collaboration

The RoundTable builds a culture of trust and inclusiveness for participants to see more of the whole and to make better decisions faster and more effectively at the lowest possible point in the organization.

Once the RoundTable methodology is in place and functioning, the CEO will manage from a view that ensures the consistent and efficient flow of authority, work, and communications activity as measured by the P&L and balance sheet. This view is generated by the BusinessLoop methodology.

The business institution's business problems occur in the human activities within the internal and external functions and in the interfaces between those functions. The BusinessLoop tool focuses on the *business entity's* challenge to coordinate separate functions.

BUSINESSLOOP
For Coordination

The **BusinessLoop** tool coordinates the functional diversity of the participants.

The BusinessLoop tool addresses the functional relationships the business institution has with its participants.

This tool for coordination provides a process and framework to apply participants' combined greater knowledge of the whole to decision making, taking into account the trade-offs between long- and short-term priorities.

Using the RoundTable tool brings clarity to the influences of the people relationships with the business institution and with the other internal and external human participants. A BusinessLoop represents the relationships that the participants have with the business institution and with the other participants. The business institution requires these relationships to support the CEO's vision for its long-term sustainability.

For better understanding of these tools—what they are and are not—in the next four chapters, we take them apart and examine them separately and then discuss how they operate together. Trust cannot be achieved by using only one or the other; both RoundTable and BusinessLoop must be understood and implemented together.

CEOs with the courage, humility, and strength of character to fully embrace an ethical, holistic, less hierarchical way of operating can use these tools to create a new environment that re-establishes the trust with the participants that has been lost.

Chapter 3

RoundTable: The Tool for Collaboration

ROUNDTABLE
For Collaboration

In Europe, I learned from Herr Braxmeir's metaphor of language, borders, cultures, that if we want people to permanently change their business behavior, just insisting on it because we are "the boss" will not be enough. Nor will saying "trust us" promote meaningful change.

Although it was slow going, the country managers and I did evolve together. We began to get in touch with the right-brain beliefs of inclusiveness, diversity, and collaboration. As RoundTabling produced clearer and more open exchanges of information by overcoming the limitations of language, borders, and cultures, we began to appreciate just how powerful a tool it could be for any CEO in any environment.

Returning from Europe, I expanded the RoundTable process to create an efficient, repeatable methodology for collecting as many diverse inputs as rapidly as possible to make the best decision for a specific issue at a specific point in time.

Changing the environment from one that benefits few to an environment of trust

A good introduction to the RoundTable tool is a comparison of how the CEO and the participants think and behave in the desired RoundTable environment compared to the thinking and business behavior of current rectangular environment.

Figure 3.1: The contrasting characteristics of the Rectangular (benefits to few) and Roundtable (trust) environments

BENEFITS TO FEW "RECTANGULAR"

- HIERARCHICAL DECISION MAKING
- INDIVIDUAL KNOWLEDGE IS POWER
- ENVIRONMENT OF FEAR
- FAILURE IS FINAL
- DEFLECT RESPONSIBILTY
- GOAL IS TO PROVE AND DEFEND
- COMPETITIVENESS

ENVIRONMENT OF TRUST "ROUNDTABLE"

- THERE IS NO "HEAD" OF THE TABLE
- SHARED KNOWLEDGE IS POWER
- ENVIRONMENT OF RESPECT
- ACCOUNTABILITY WITHOUT SHAME
- COLLABORATION & COOPERATION
- DECISION MAKING AT THE APPROPRIATE LEVEL
- OPEN COMMUNICATIONS

The CEO believes falsely that CEOs can and must always be in "total control." Friction is experienced without participants recognizing the cause. In this environment participants deflect responsibility to protect themselves from blame. Operating reviews, PowerPoint™ presentations, finger pointing, and self-justification are more important than solving business issues to the ultimate detriment of the business institution's performance and long-term sustainability.

At the RoundTable, the CEO speaks his thoughts and beliefs openly and then behaves accordingly. In this environment it is safe for anyone and everyone to express their thoughts. This allows all participants to develop enough trust to contribute to prioritizing and making their collective and individual decisions for the good of the business institution and all of the participants instead of focusing on their individual special interests. Participants respond with decisive, purposeful action through collaboration.

Regardless of its industry or size, the long-term success or failure of every business is determined by the relationships of people with people. Even if we could entirely rely on robots to produce our products and services, we wouldn't have robots buying our products, investing in our businesses, managing our customers' problems, or running our communities and governments. So, at least for the foreseeable future, business institutions will continue to rely on people relating to people. That is why people relationships must always be the CEO's primary focus as he pursues his vision for his number-one responsibility, which is the sustainability of the institution.

The *people benefit* of the RoundTable methodology is to have all participants share their knowledge supported by a respectful, trusting environment as they pursue their individual financial and personal expectations and deliver on their individual commitments.

The *business benefit* of the RoundTable methodology is informed, rapid decision making and implementation through holistic thinking and collaboration for the long-term sustainability of the business. This considers the impact of all decisions on revenue, cost, and on all participants over time and not just in the short-term.

Convening a RoundTable

There is not one RoundTable. There are many—each based on an identified and agreed-upon issue requiring collaboration of the participants. The process of calling and setting a RoundTable follows a regimen and is not done arbitrarily. Any participant can express the desire for an issue or opportunity to be addressed at a RoundTable; however, it takes appropriate authority to convene a table.

If it is within a function, the line manager makes the call. If it appears to be cross-functional, the appropriate level of management decides whether or not to bring the people resources from multiple functions together to form a RoundTable. Before calling a RoundTable, agree to enough facts to avoid wasting resources and time.

Once the RoundTable is formed, the participants are *not* chosen based on who reports to whom on the organization chart. The responsibility and authority to make and implement *functional* decisions follows the reporting structure of the organizational chart. The responsibility and authority to make *cross-functional* decisions flows non-hierarchically through the RoundTable process instead of through the hierarchical levels and reporting relationships of the organizational chart.

The issue leader of a particular RoundTable calls together those participants from the levels and layers of the organization whose functional responsibilities are at the closest point to the issue or opportunity. A second-level manager from one function could be sitting next to a line worker from another layer of the organization. This is where the issue is most clearly felt, best known and understood, and can be addressed with the maximum creativity and efficiency.

The RoundTable process does not dispute that every business institution needs to have an orderly and formal organizational structure. You cannot do away with the organization chart. But it is counterproductive to use the organization chart to prescribe the flow of authority for rapid and efficient cross-functional decision making and problem resolution. The RoundTable process aligns individuals to contribute from their expertise and responsibility as parts of the whole business institution rather than as functional silos.

Line managers must now accept, create, and protect an environment that allows their direct reports to participate in making cross-functional business decisions without requiring line approval as long as those decisions are made by following the RoundTable and BusinessLoop methodologies. Since the structural approach to authority is so embedded in the culture of many business institutions, the CEO might be the only one who can institute and enforce the RoundTable process for this new environment of efficient decision making and rapid implementation.

Trust and the continuum of perspectives

Trust is a pre-requisite for the RoundTable to work. Participants must trust that their leadership wants and supports decisions based on the new beliefs of long-term sustainability, connectedness, and inclusion, and not on the old beliefs encompassed in the benefit-to-few environment. If participants do not trust that this is so, they will try to block the implementation of the CEO's vision—aggressively or passively—or just run for the hills. Without the participants trusting and delivering on their commitments, the institution will fail to live to the full extent of its DNA.

For a CEO to rebuild trust, all participants must believe that their needs, desires, and expectations are being taken into account. This does not mean that everyone or every special interest is going to get what they want. That can never happen. Participants know that, whether they admit it or not. It does mean that participants come to believe that their individual and collective needs, desires, and expectations will be considered in the CEO's framework of the business institution's long-term sustainability along with all other participants. The long-term sustainability of the business institution is the CEO's standard for decision making, not special interests or favoritism.

So how does the CEO get participants to change their old beliefs to these? The starting point is to lead participants to recognize that all individual perspectives occur on a continuum. You can't accomplish this understanding if people's behavior is attacking or disrespectful. One of the first steps in the RoundTable process is to establish new ground rules of business behavior that allow people to share their perspectives while requiring everyone else to listen.

Apply RoundTable etiquette and behavior any time two or more people interact. It becomes the standard for how people in the organization treat each other—with dignity, respect and inclusiveness—whether they are seated at a RoundTable or passing in the parking lot.

Figure 3.2: RoundTable Behavior and Etiquette

ROUNDTABLE BEHAVIOR AND ETIQUETTE
• ROUNDTABLE ETIQUETTE IS RESPECTFUL AND INCLUSIVE. • THE ENVIRONMENT IS ONE OF OPENNESS AND TRUST. • PARTICIPANTS COME WITH A COMMITTMENT TO THE PROCESS. • THIS IS THE TIME TO SHOW PASSION AND BE ADAMANT ABOUT YOUR KNOWLEDGE ON A TOPIC. • PARTICIPANTS DIRECT THEIR PASSION AT THE TOPIC IN THE CENTER OF THE ROUNDTABLE AND NOT AT ANOTHER PERSON.

In most issues or disagreements, people defend opposing points of view as if those were the only perspectives. In the RoundTable environment, participants learn to appreciate that many diverse points of view appropriately exist. They accept that opposing perspectives exist on a continuum with others existing in between and on either side.

The CEO's behavior demonstrates that no single perspective is correct over the other, creating an environment where participants begin to experiment with changing their own beliefs. Those who are not willing to change find that through the methodology of the RoundTable process, the CEO requires them to change their behavior, whether they change their beliefs or not.

CEO MOMENT #4
All problems and all possible choices exist on continuums. There is no perfect understanding of any issue and, therefore, no perfect solution. There is only choice.

CEO MOMENT

RoundTable participants don't waste time and resources looking for the "perfect solution" or even believing that it exists. They know that it doesn't. There can be different choices, each effective in its own way. The business institution gains value as participants aggregate their diverse personal perspectives and shift their focus from how they are affected as individuals to a perspective that considers the impact to the institution and all of the participants.

The more participants recognize that they operate on a shared continuum, the more they experience the connection of being part of a larger whole. They not only feel better, they mentally open up to making the types of decisions that support the institution's ability to operate toward long-term sustainability as it delivers on their expectations.

In the RoundTable environment, it becomes accepted and acceptable that being on a continuum will more often show differences in perspective than alignment. The differences are called out and discussed. This doesn't mean that decisions are made through consensus. Rather, at the RoundTable participants become willing to trust in each other's behaviors, trust in the CEO's and other leaders' integrity, and trust in the RoundTable process to balance the participants' desires and the institution's needs. We know that trust has become widespread and that the RoundTable is really working when individuals are comfortable knowing that even in their absence the rest of the group will take their positions into account.

This trust can only come about through shared beliefs driving consistent business behavior and when every individual and interest group is, and feels, considered and included in the prioritization and decision-making process, regardless of the timing of their expectations being met.

RoundTable requires the levels of the organization to give up knowing all the details

Every participant in every layer of a business institution has the responsibility for some appropriate level of daily detail given his or her function, and every detail of every activity is the appropriate responsibility of someone. Whether it is the CEO or the person on the production line, it is not required, necessary, desirable, or even possible for any one person or group of people in any business institution to be on top of every participant's detail.

As CEO, you cannot be in the detail of every activity. You hire people you trust and assign them the responsibility to perform the details of their function daily. This is true whether the environment is RoundTable or rectangular.

In the RoundTable environment, the CEO believes that he is responsible to address the details of making sure that all participants stay connected and that relationships are respectfully built on mutual trust. The CEO believes that participants in the levels and layers of the organization understand better than anyone else the conditions and details of their functions and their responsibilities. As long as the participants follow the RoundTable process to be inclusive and use the BusinessLoop process to see the operational connections, they have the authority to make decisions and act.

Here's what's been accomplished at the RoundTable so far.

- We've collected the appropriate participants from all levels of the organization.

- We've teed up a business problem and given participants the authority to solve it.

- We've released the tyranny of the "perfect solution."

- Participants are starting to express their perspectives without threat or fear.

- We've introduced the method of improving communications through re-expressing another person's point of view.

Now that we agree that perspectives exist on a shared continuum, our problems are solved. Yeah, right!

Appreciating the continuum of thought doesn't preclude disagreements and misunderstandings on tactics and actions. When disagreements arise, the RoundTable appreciation of a continuum of different perspectives is a touchstone to return us to a point where we are in agreement and collaborating.

A collaborative culture doesn't just happen. The CEO and the management team must create and protect it. Desire for this culture expressed through speaking or memos is not enough to create it. To change the environment to support this new collaborative culture of dialogue, the CEO must model the behavior that he wants and expects.

If participants get lost or have disagreements, they stay grounded by asking:

- What is the effect of this perspective on the institution's revenue over time?

- What is the effect of this perspective on the institution's cost over time?

- What is the effect of this perspective on each and all participants over time?

CEO MOMENT #5
When disagreements happen, the collaborative culture directs us to return to where we had agreement.

CEO MOMENT

As participants tackle business issues and opportunities, there will be disagreements most often caused by confusion over what is being said, what is being heard, and intentions (real or perceived). Two hurdles that must be overcome for effectively implementing the RoundTable methodology are *dialogue vs. debate* and *content vs. envelope*.

Dialogue vs. debate

The RoundTable methodology is based on dialogue not debate. The difference is not subtle. It is huge but not always obvious.

A dialogue is an engagement for the purpose of finding the truth about a particular issue or topic. Participants come at it with facts as they know them. They are open to finding the truth by engaging in dialogue to find facts that they don't know or to see the facts they do know from a different perspective.

In a debate participants assume that they have all the facts, have interpreted facts correctly, and know the truth. They are trying to prove themselves right and convince or prove that the other person is wrong.

Dialoguing is not for delaying decisions. Dialoguing does not replace or remove the responsibility for achieving goals. Dialoguing is for faster more effective decision making and for improving the cycle time of implementation. Along with being able to speak and be heard, comes the accountability of making and supporting the decisions from this process.

The CEO demonstrates by words and actions that the Round-Table methodology is not bureaucratic consensus management. The RoundTable participants agree up front on who is responsible for making the final decision and what inputs are required. The person making the decision will change depending on the issue being discussed.

Content vs. envelope

When functions in a business institution are not working together, a big part of the reason is that some participants, individually and in groups, hold beliefs about each other that get in the way of mutual respect. When someone doesn't respect a person for whatever reason, he tends to minimize the output of the function that person performs and discounts whatever that person has to say.

In any communication between people, there is the "content" and there is the "envelope." The content is internal to the participant—the fact or issue that the communication is about as the participant holding it believes it to be. The envelope is external—the participants' physical behaviors, the inflections, the words they choose, what is being said, and what is being done.

In the first stages of RoundTabling, participants become aware of how the issues and facts of the content can be confused with the characteristics of the envelope. The benefits of the RoundTable are realized when the confusion between the content and the envelope is resolved.

The envelope is dual, meaning that it is created by both the sender and the receiver. It is what people see and sense, what they are taking in directly through their eyes, ears, and intuition. The sender contributes to the envelope by his words and body language; the receiver defines the envelope by what he perceives through his own filters of beliefs and experience.

Using experts to overcome hurdles in the RoundTable process

When implementing the RoundTable process, an *industrial psychologist* and a *trained meeting facilitator* will help address the reality of human variability. These trusted experts are especially important when you are first introducing the RoundTable methodology into your company. Choose experts who have your confidence, and then consistently apply their approaches and tools to make the RoundTable part of your business's way of doing things.

CEO MOMENT #6
Trusted experts help overcome the hurdles of Content vs. Envelope and Dialogue vs. Debate.

CEO MOMENT

The industrial psychologist introduces participants to the concepts of content versus envelope and dialogue verses debate. Participants get to know and trust each other as people by discussing the beliefs behind their behavior versus the facts being discussed. If this sounds a little touchy-feely, it isn't.

You, as CEO, are not going to entrust your authority to people to make decisions and use company resources until you understand what drives their behavior and trust that they will follow the RoundTable process. Participants won't trust you until you operate consistently with integrity by aligning your thoughts, words, and behavior.

The objective of relationship building isn't to make the participants feel good about themselves and others, although that is often a reward. The objective is to make the most efficient use of the participants' time when communicating to make rapid and informed decisions for the business and to give them the authority to execute them. The value-add of the industrial psychologist is to hold up a mirror so that participants can see the reflection of their behavior and challenge themselves by asking, is this really truth-seeking behavior, or is it driven by some inside belief that I hold about the other person or myself?

Participants begin to appreciate the impact that content and envelope have on communications and cooperation. Once participants are aware of the content/envelope confusion and begin to take responsibility for their own envelopes, the CEO will not need an industrial psychologist at every RoundTable. This does not mean that envelopes will never appear again. It does mean that they become less and less a hurdle to rapid and informed decision making.

A *meeting facilitator*, whether an external expert or an internal employee, is an ongoing requirement for all RoundTables. The RoundTable facilitator focuses on the content thanks to the work the industrial psychologist did to dampen the fire and heat generated by conflicting personalities confusing the envelope and the content.

Figure 3.3: RoundTable Ground Rules

GROUND RULES FOR CONDUCTING A ROUNDTABLE

- IS THE ISSUE AND/OR OPPORTUNITY OPENLY EXPRESSED WITH ENOUGH SPECIFICITY FOR PARTICIPANTS TO AGREE THAT THIS IS A PRIORITY WORTH BEING ADDRESSED NOW?
- IF SO, THE ISSUE OWNER CONVENES THE TABLE.
- THE ISSUE OWNER ASKS QUESTIONS TO DETERMINE WHO NEEDS TO BE AT THE ROUNDTABLE.
  - WHY IS THIS AN ISSUE, PROBLEM OR OPPORTUNITY?
  - WHO IS IN THE BEST POSITION TO MAKE THE DECISION?
  - WHO AFFECTS OR IS AFFECTED BY THIS ISSUE AND HOW?
  - HOW ARE THE FINANCIAL MEASUREMENTS, P&LS, AND BALANCE SHEET AFFECTED?
- THE MEETING FACILITATOR LEADS THE DISCUSSION AND CAPTURES INFORMATION.
- ALL PARTICIPANTS FOLLOW ROUNDTABLE ETIQUETTE AND BEHAVIOR.
- EVERY ROUNDTABLE ALWAYS RESULTS IN A DECISION AND ACTION, WITH RESOURCES EITHER ASSIGNED OR REMOVED.

A good facilitator takes RoundTabling to the next level by producing the most effective use of formal and informal group dialogue. Whether twenty people are preparing a financial forecast in a conference room or two people are talking at the water cooler, we expect a consistency in the way they behave and treat each other that identifies content or envelope and conforms to the standard of dialogue not debate.

ARDIS: Language, borders, cultures, American-style

About a year after returning from Europe, I became the CEO of ARDIS, a struggling wireless data network that was a joint venture of Motorola and IBM. Eager to bring the RoundTable methodology into this company, I believed that without the added burden of LBC, it would be much easier to implement new ideas than it had been in Europe.

Talk about having to change my own beliefs!

Although the participants at this start-up shared the same language and culture, the business functions' borders were monolithic in the same way that the countries of Europe had been. In Europe, we were dealing with LBC. Back in the United States with the start-up, the separateness of country-think was replaced by the separateness of function-think.

As it turned out, this environment, with functions and business units acting more like silos than part of a singular business institution, could not have been a more fertile ground for exercising and improving the tools that supported my new beliefs of leadership. The founding management team and about a third of the employees came from high-performance environments where organizational flow and hierarchical authority structures were well established, and where participants understood how decisions were made hierarchically.

ARDIS had the uniqueness of in-building wireless coverage, an advanced capability for the early nineties; this was prior to the explosion of cell-phone coverage and texting. The organization took naturally to institutional processes and Six Sigma quality management. Employees had an unusually high level of commitment to their customers. Participants were hired for their functional expertise and were competent and capable.

However, appreciation for the linkages between the functions was missing. This lack of appreciation contributed to the problems of the business. When issues arose, the participants in the various functional silos would not acknowledge that they needed input from participants in other silos. They wouldn't admit that their decisions and output affected other functions and, therefore, the business institution as a whole. This lack of understanding of content and envelope was apparent in people's behavior.

In spite of having committed participants, loyal customers, adequate funding from IBM and Motorola, and a technology that was more advanced than any other data technology then in the marketplace, ARDIS missed its revenue and expense commitments two years in a row. If my predecessor had a vision for long-term sustainability, it certainly wasn't shared and agreed upon by the people in the functions or by IBM and Motorola as the investors and members of the Board.

Instead of working together to build a new company, the various functions used their expertise as shields to resist coming together. Each function defended its budget and performance without focusing on the total business' performance. Relationships between the functions had deteriorated to such a point that the manager of engineering and operations installed inside locks on the doors between his organization and the rest of the company.

The RoundTable takes hold at ARDIS

Because of the lessons learned from LBC in Europe, introducing the RoundTable was my first action at ARDIS. With the assistance of an industrial psychologist, the management team met off-site to focus on what it would take for ARDIS to successfully reach its full DNA.

I was confident that we could optimize ARDIS's sustainability if we could change the current environment to one of appreciation and respect for diversity. All participants needed to recognize that no one person or function could see the whole.

The management team at ARDIS understood authority and functional responsibility. We used this understanding along with the RoundTable process to get them working together. Even if there wasn't friendship, there would be the opportunity for observing each other's competence and eventually developing respect and appreciation for what each brought functionally to the business and to our customers.

My direct reports' first reaction to the offsite meeting was, oh no, another team-building exercise. To them, this was the mental version of group bungee jumping while hoping their cord was not the one to break. As they would learn, a RoundTable offsite is not about team building or bungee jumping. It is about knitting together many different participants and activities that, when coordinated, deliver the business institution's products and services.

Instead of focusing on the aggregated ability of the team first, as they expected, we focused on the diversity of the functions, the individuals within them, and what each uniquely brought to the whole. The emphasis on differences and individuality is a way to challenge and deconstruct the assumptions that people make about each other. It causes people to recognize attributes in others that they didn't recognize before.

It didn't take many hours of observing my direct reports "trading envelopes" for me to see that the participants were getting down to the content inside.

The irony was that the employees within the functions were exceptionally qualified, competent, and committed to performing. Managers recognized these qualities in their own functions, but distrust, false assumptions, and misunderstandings caused them *not* to recognize these qualities in the other functions. Uncoordinated functional activities failed to give the business institution its complete value and kept it from being able to live up to its full DNA.

RoundTabling and quality function linked

Janet P., our quality manager at ARDIS, quickly embraced the RoundTable and helped me recognize that the quality function was a natural place for the facilitation responsibility to reside. She welcomed the assignment.

Janet already was good at focusing on the steps to identifying problems, finding possible options, making effective decisions, allocating resources, and implementing. She had an instinct for separating envelopes from the content and participants' words from the beliefs that drove their behavior.

Janet demonstrated a calm manner that brought to light as much of the truth on the issue as possible. She quickly extended the momentum that the industrial psychologist had established by guiding people in RoundTables to become acclimated to collaborative meeting behavior.

A breakthrough happened at ARDIS when the engineering manager said he didn't believe something the marketing manager said. As soon as he uttered the words, "I don't believe you; you are lying," everyone in the room froze. Everyone, that is except Janet, who, as facilitator, held to the process and didn't grade the envelope or the content.

Instead, she calmly asked, "What about this don't you believe? Is it the content or is it envelope?" As she made all the participants at the RoundTable hold still for the discussion that followed—which took some time and serious facilitating—it became clear that while what the marketing manager said wasn't necessarily factual, she believed it and behaved accordingly.

Since the engineering manager didn't believe her facts, he assumed the marketing manager didn't believe them either and was intentionally lying. With everything out in the open, the participants offered their feedback in front of the group. Janet ensured that it was delivered in an even-handed manner that was respectful to all. The power was in getting people to share what they were thinking at the RoundTable and not hold it back if it was going to drive their behavior. If there was something to be said positive or negative, it was good for all to hear.

Janet P.'s litmus test to differentiate between content and envelope:

- Are the participants dialoguing to find the true facts (content) or debating to prove their own observation is correct and that the other person is wrong (envelope)?

- Are the participants valuing the other person's point of view (content)?

- Is one participant attacking the other person (envelope) as a way of disagreeing with that person's point of view (content)?

The RoundTable facilitator is surely concerned about the people, but her role isn't to resolve the envelope. It is to handle the business issues contained in the content inside the envelopes. As facilitator, if Janet saw that the issue was envelope and couldn't be quickly resolved, she didn't hesitate to bring in "envelope" resources, such as our human resource manager, or to bring back the industrial psychologist.

As the RoundTable moved from envelope to content issues, Janet kept the process on track by capturing the information about business issues on flipcharts. Even in this day of laptops and PowerPoint™ charts with screen sharing, I still like to use flipcharts or smart boards in RoundTables. There is something powerful about participants picking up a marker and physically expressing their views for everyone in the room to see.

CEO MOMENT #7
Visual aids, such as flip charts or smart boards, are important devices to create the linkage between RoundTable and BusinessLoop tools.

CEO MOMENT

As a quality manager, Janet had a sense of a RoundTable issue's impact on the rest of the organization because of her quality training. Seeing how one particular RoundTable issue could be affected by another RoundTable issue, she was able to cross-migrate issues that weren't table specific but affected another part of the company. That turned into a huge benefit.

By using Janet as our first in-house facilitator instead of continuing to use an expert from the outside the company, ARDIS retained the institutional learning as Janet moved from Round-Table to RoundTable. In the beginning her RoundTable role overshadowed her other responsibilities. Eventually as more participants went through the RoundTable process, Janet trained co-workers to be facilitators along with their functional roles, thereby migrating her expertise to others in the company.

There are many qualified experts in industrial psychology and meeting facilitation. The chosen trusted experts will be an extension of the CEO, so it is critical to choose wisely. Early RoundTables set the slope of people's learning curve, so be thoughtful, and select experts who have earned your confidence and with whom you are strongly connected.

Establish the RoundTable ground rules for conducting meetings and then be consistent in adhering to these. Do not delegate the definition of meeting process, etiquette, and behavior to anyone else. This is the CEO's first step in implementing the desired culture change that opens the door to the benefits that the Round-Table brings.

I can't say that the introduction of the RoundTable methodology to ARDIS achieved an immediate acceptance. Far from it, but at least the functional managers understood that they were expected to treat each other with dignity and respect rather than lob hand grenades over the transom or fight like a group of Rottweilers.

We rapidly moved from focusing on internal issues and conflict to focusing on the business issues facing ARDIS. For the first time, the company met its financial forecasts.

Questions to help your personal reflections.

CEO REFLECTIONS

These questions helped the managers at ARDIS understand how personal beliefs affect business issues by driving business behaviors.

- Is this a high priority issue? For whom? You? Your function? The business? Why?

- Is there a lack of trust between the functions in your organization?

- Is this lack of trust about content or the envelope?

- Is it affecting how decisions are made?

- Is it affecting profitability and/or customer satisfaction?

- How would your organization respond to the ground rules and etiquette in Figures 3.2 and 3.3?

From ARDIS, I moved to a new international assignment, where it didn't take long for another case study to present itself.

Chapter 4

The RoundTable in Action

ROUNDTABLE
For Collaboration

In the mid-nineties, the cellular communications business was exploding country by country across the globe. With responsibility for Motorola's multi-billion dollar cellular device business in North and South America, I had multiple country managers managing P&Ls in markets as diverse as Canada, Brazil, and the United States.

In most cases, the same cellular device could be sold across borders. This was a good thing for manufacturers, but the counterpoint was that we had to be very careful with pricing because products were beginning to migrate across borders, either legally with tariffs or in other ways as distributors dishonored their territory agreements.

Each country manager that reported to me was driven by satisfying his in-country network operators and by achieving his own performance and financial measurements. Each was expert at understanding his own individual markets. None of them appreciated the diversity of the others' markets. None of them looked at the business as a whole.

What was seen as a good order and worthy of attractive pricing in one market was viewed as a small order deserving little discount in another. We could set a precedent price in a small market and try to keep it quiet since it wasn't a legal issue, but the minute a larger network operator became aware, he would start hammering for deeper discount based on his greater volume. Therefore, individual market pricing for the same product had significant impact on the price offered in all other markets.

A tremendous number of initial cell phone manufacturers couldn't survive the pricing pressure. Many well-respected quality brands came and went. The manufacturers who were going to survive and make a business out of it had to become hyper-sensitive to their margins and volumes and manage inside this environment of shifting pressures and special interests that they couldn't control.

Managing pricing through the RoundTable process

I had inherited a huge hub-and-spoke process. The country managers were used to coming to my predecessor for order-by-order pricing as a series of one-off decisions based on the volume and what price and terms were needed to close the particular order of the day. There had been some situational sensitivity to the effect that pricing could have on new volumes but little consideration of the long-term effect of pricing decisions on the business or on *all* participants.

Pricing affected all functions of the business and the total P&L. Since this was my responsibility, I convened a RoundTable to address the pricing issue.

Before this we had successfully used the RoundTable methodology on less complex issues and opportunities, including product warranty with good results. At least the managers did understand the methodology and had seen benefits in other areas of the business. However, changing from a rectangular to the RoundTable environment is never easy.

Regardless of the issues or business environment, it always takes considerable and consistent effort on the part of the CEO for participants to believe and accept that we were all going to follow the RoundTable process to make decisions for carrying out our responsibilities. This wasn't any different with this group.

CEO MOMENT #8
If you adopt the RoundTable methodology, it must be followed without exception, at the water cooler, in the halls, in meetings, and in all other communications and decision-making situations.

CEO MOMENT

Every perspective must be out in the open instead of being driven underground. My direct reports knew that I expected their business behavior to align with the RoundTable ground rules and etiquette, whether their personal beliefs had evolved or not. Some of them were beginning to establish trust with me and, to a lesser extent, with each other. Addressing the pricing issue gave us the opportunity to apply the RoundTable methodology to an issue that touched all parts of the business and was causing problems for all the country managers, no matter the size or conditions of their markets.

The pricing RoundTable convenes

Everyone traveled to the first pricing RoundTable meeting. Country managers, sales managers, finance, legal, engineering, and production people from all over the Americas arrived. As the initiator and issue owner of pricing RoundTable, I wrote the following on the board:

WHAT SHOULD OUR PRICING STRATEGY BE?
HOW WILL WE ARRIVE AT IT?

I opened the discussion by asking participants which variables would drive our pricing decisions order by order and over time.

After years in a rectangular environment with a leader who managed by hub and spoke and sought to be in control, some of the participants in the pricing RoundTable at first sat at the table without speaking, in their own way holding back from participating in the RoundTable process.

For some of them, fear and lack of trust were driving this behavior. Others didn't believe that their input was really valued in making decisions. For others, the old belief of knowledge is power, knowledge is king was operating. Those who retained this old belief resisted participating in the environment of inclusion, trust, and openness that the RoundTable can create. They thought that if they freely shared what they knew, they wouldn't be seen as better than their peers. They feared they wouldn't be recognized with a promotion, a raise, or increased responsibility. They didn't want to be part of the whole; they wanted to be viewed as better than their peers because that was how they had achieved recognition in the past rectangular table environment.

As issue owner, I held the group to the RoundTable process of content and envelope. Hidden beliefs and envelope behavior that opposed the RoundTable culture became visible. Participants were required to listen and consider every point, no matter how diverse or at odds it was with their own.

The RoundTable didn't permit second-guessing another person's intent even though it might appear that the speaker was naïve, self-motivated, or even badly intended. In all properly executed RoundTables, if the participant is naïve, the process will educate him. If the person is self-motivated or badly intended, that will come out too.

This wasn't a problem at the pricing roundtable. If it had been, as table leader, I would have asked the offending participant to leave the table. Then in private I would have coached, reprimanded or, if worse came to worst, terminated him for being unwilling to follow the RoundTable methodology.

Respect for the diversity of others' thoughts is the outgrowth of accepting that no one person, not even the CEO, sees the whole or has total control. This is difficult to accept in today's business environment, so some participants may begin by just giving lip service to this new belief. But by staying with the RoundTable methodology for meeting behavior, well-intended participants will see and trust this new belief of having choice not control.

Working the RoundTable process through content versus envelope

As is so often the case in RoundTabling, the pricing Table used specific business events—individual orders from network operators for cellular phones—as an effective way to illuminate specific sub-issues of pricing. Once people started opening up, to say there was a continuum of perspectives at the pricing RoundTable was an understatement. There were participants who didn't want to hear the perspective of others or remember that they were part of a larger whole. It had been one thing to RoundTable on product warranty, but pricing was much more of a lightening rod.

It became clear around the Roundtable, as it always does, when someone was responding to another participant's envelope instead of the content of the business issues. I continually had to keep the dialogue directed at the content.

The content discussion at the RoundTable identified key variables: current products versus next generation products, product cost, competitive pricing, learning curves, inventory, market size, and potential. Many issues and learned experiences were put on the table, coming from many diverse points of view.

After staying with it, the participants at the pricing RoundTable, although from multiple countries and affected by different economies, markets, customers, and regulatory policies, began to recognize where we shared agreement and where we didn't. We agreed on taking appropriate care of the customers, dealing with current and future competitors, and addressing current and future P&L commitments to the company.

We also agreed upon where we disagreed. The sticking point was how to arrive at the very specific price for small markets versus large markets and small orders versus very large orders, and then how to explain the pricing process to the affected customers, with their own special interests.

The pricing RoundTable participants began to aggregate their diverse inputs to create a more complete view of the whole pricing issue for more effective and rapid decision making and implementation. These managers used the excellent methodology of scenario planning to have the discussion about future pricing.

They agreed to these priorities in this order:

- The company's long-term sustainability, which included current and future P&L impact,

- The customer,

- The distribution channel, and

- The individual internal measurements of the internal participants.

Using actual events, the RoundTable established how pricing decisions would be made going forward in a consistent and coordinated manner. To reach a decision and take action, the country managers at the pricing RoundTable had to compromise. As you would expect, the larger markets and larger orders were afforded a larger coefficient of influence than the smaller markets. The strategy included quantity discounts, strategic discounts, and end of model life discounts. Generally, larger markets and orders would receive more favorable treatment.

The bigger markets felt better about the new pricing strategy than their counterparts in smaller markets, but for the most part, everyone, even the smaller country managers, thought the new pricing strategy and process would work to the greatest good of the whole addressing the cross border pricing issues. Those who had been reluctant at first soon saw the benefit of our strategy. They were confident that I meant what I said when I told them that the business would support them in implementing the pricing strategy we set.

The RoundTable participants had addressed the questions I had written on the board. We had our pricing strategy and assigned human and capital resources to carry it out. This replaced the one-off pricing strategy that had been in place. We next had to consider the effect of our new pricing strategy on internal measurements and compensation. Although the pricing RoundTable participants had agreed that they did not want pricing decisions to be driven by internal measurements if those measurements would compromise either the company or the customers, their compensation and measurement remained a valid concern that needed to be addressed. The RoundTable methodology doesn't automatically make these issues go away.

After months of being open about my business beliefs and consistently supporting those beliefs with my behavior, I had established a level of trust with them. When I acknowledged that making people at least neutral on their measurements and compensation when they acted in the best interest of the whole was a desirable goal, the participants at the RoundTable believed me, if a bit reluctantly, trusting that I would address the measurement issue when the time came.

The RoundTable methodology will produce dialogue that drives decisions and creates output

The pricing RoundTable worked out tremendously. The country managers and CFOs left with a shared sense of trust and the truth as best they could see it. During the RoundTable process they had gained insight as to why we would no longer engage in a one-off pricing strategy given the destructive effect that was having on total company revenues and customer relationships.

The participants in the North Americas pricing RoundTable understood that it was their responsibility to return to their functions and countries and convey how pricing decisions would be made in the future.

I felt a great sense of accomplishment. Now it was up to the participants to implement what we had agreed on and communicate back to their individual organizations. We all felt that this was a great moment of progress, and it was. But, as the new belief states, we have choice, not control. In a later chapter, we will see that even though the RoundTable pricing was a success, one individual can make a choice that can derail the process.

Communicating RoundTable decisions to the rest of the organization

Like any existing business, we had a process for sharing information throughout the company when decisions were made. We used this existing process as a starting point for communications between the pricing RoundTable and the rest of the organization.

Imagine the country manager of Canada sitting at the pricing RoundTable and metaphorically swiveling his chair around. His counterparts from Brazil and Mexico along with the functional managers of production, engineering, and sales do the same.

As each participant swivels around, he or she intersects with a different collection of participants at another table. Those other tables could be the country's sales forecast RoundTable, a customer issues RoundTable, or a RoundTable dealing with the functions of production and design.

Whatever the subjects of other Roundtables were, they may have impacted or been impacted by pricing, but their issues were other than pricing. RoundTables gain knowledge from and share knowledge back with other RoundTables. They do not overlap nor are they isolated islands of decision making.

Ownership of the pricing issue was given to the CFO. The country managers worked with their peers, staffs, and subordinates to follow the RoundTable methodology while implementing our agreed-upon pricing strategy in their countries and markets.

The purpose of the RoundTable is to make better decisions faster and more effectively at the lowest point in the organization. It also becomes a tool for teaching how to treat each other with dignity and respect.

CEO MOMENT #9
The RoundTable methodology creates an environment that authorizes and supports decision making at the appropriate point in the organization.

CEO MOMENT

I wanted the organization to become equipped and capable of taking action without waiting for my approval. This can happen only when decision making has been decentralized by trusting that the people at the point of the issue have the tools and processes to make the best choice given the facts that are known for the business's long- and short-term interests.

Participants won't make decisions this way if they don't trust or feel trusted. They must believe that the CEO can be trusted to support them if they follow RoundTable decision making, and they will have her support and the authority to act.

Daily choices made in managing the business will always be made with less than complete information. Mistakes and failures are certain to occur. The RoundTable way of operating recognizes these hurdles.

Fear of the ramifications of failure can cause participants to stay too long with ineffective decisions. They will use debate not dialogue and envelope not content, wasting precious time defending actions and deflecting responsibility for a non-yielding tactic while losing sight of the greater objective.

We wanted the pricing RoundTable to put the effort into making intelligent decisions and assessing the results, and then keep going. The goal was to make rapid, inclusive decisions followed by actions that would yield results that might not be perfect.

We knew the RoundTable was taking hold. When something changed, the impacted functions returned to use the process again. If the decision didn't yield the results they wanted, they learned from it and tried something else.

"Take a method and try it. If it fails, admit it and try another. But above all, try something."

— Franklin D. Roosevelt, President of the United States

When the participants embrace the RoundTable methodology and supporting beliefs immediately, it is personally healthy for them and optimal for the business. In the beginning the requirement is not so much to have participants embrace it as it is to have them behave it.

- Now that you've been through the RoundTable chapters, how would your staff meetings change as they evolve from being conducted in a rectangular environment to a RoundTable environment?

- Can you see where the RoundTable methodology could help participants knock down barriers in their personal relationships that get in the way of business success?

- Do you see how the RoundTable methodology could make it possible to align functional activities and measurements in rebuilding trust?

- Can you see how short-term measurements drive decisions that damage the long-term sustainability of the business institution?

- How would the measurement system in your company support the concepts of the RoundTable?

In Chapters 3 and 4, we talked about collaboration and cooperation among participants to prioritize and deal with the content of business issues and opportunities without being distracted by the envelope.

In Chapters 5 and 6 we add the BusinessLoop tool to the RoundTable methodology to order and coordinate the business functions as they address the content of the business issue and opportunity.

Chapter 5

BusinessLoop: The Tool for Coordination

BUSINESSLOOP
For Coordination

We just finished explaining the right brain tool of RoundTable for relationships of people to people. We now go to the left brain tool for the relationships of people to the business institution. This is the pragmatic perspective, the nuts and bolts of how decisions get made as products get built and services get delivered to achieve the CEO's vision for the institution's long-term sustainability. It is the broader frame, bigger picture, and greater expansiveness of the connections of all the participants.

The BusinessLoop tool ties the right brain RoundTable learning with the left brain activities of doing as measured by the P&L and balance sheet. Every decision is evaluated by how it will affect revenue, cost, and people over time.

A BusinessLoop is comprised of Business Flow and Relationship Flow

A BusinessLoop has two components. First is the unique Business Flow of the institution. The second is the unique Relationship Flow with all the participants as the Business Flow is implemented.

The terms Business Flow and Relationship Flow apply to any business process mapping tools you choose to use. It doesn't matter which process mapping tools you choose. What matters is that you commit to mapping the flow of the business with the relationships of the participants.

The Business Flow component of the BusinessLoop tool

Begin by having your direct reports create a business process map for your specific business that participants can point to as they are giving their perspectives on the opportunity, issue, or problem they are focusing on.

Figure 5.1: Simple Business Flow

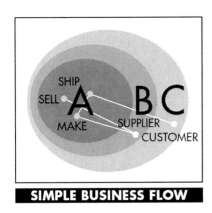

SIMPLE BUSINESS FLOW

Figure 5.1 begins inside its own company environment (A), interfaces with suppliers and business partners in environment (B), and then interfaces with customers, community, and competition in environment (C).

A Business Flow shows the activities between all participants, both internal and external, as they deliver on their commitments to the business institution. The connections between these agreed upon activities are represented by solid, linear lines. These interfaces between the environments are always in play, so that as people perform their day-to-day business activities, this is a constant visual reminder that they are affected by someone's activities up stream and their actions affect someone downstream.

Three systems operate inside every Business Flow

In every business institution, there are three independent systems: organizational structure, work systems, and communications systems. Everything that happens in a business happens in one or more of these systems. At its most complete, a Business Flow map would detail all the activities in the systems of work and communications as they interact with the organizational structure.

- **Organizational Structure:** The reporting structure and pattern of formally delegated decision making as represented in the organization chart.

- **Work Systems:** Functional expertise, competencies, and responsibilities.

- **Communications Systems:** The data and information that move between functions, throughout the levels and layers within the organization, and to all external participants and institutions.

Although viewed as independent eventually these systems intersect and overlap at the interfaces where the humans interact. These relationships, especially when they intersect at the interfaces, need to be in the forefront of everyone's mind as they go about their day-to-day responsibilities in the functional aspects of the business. This is accomplished by adhering to the RoundTable etiquette and behavior. (Figure 3.2)

The Three Systems: Organizational Structure

Until a business institution has RoundTable and BusinessLoop tools, most models have the authority for making *all* decisions flow through the levels of the *Organizational Structure* (Figure 5.2). Approvals are required from supervisors at multiple levels before decisions can be made.

Figure 5.2: Traditional organizational view of the business institution

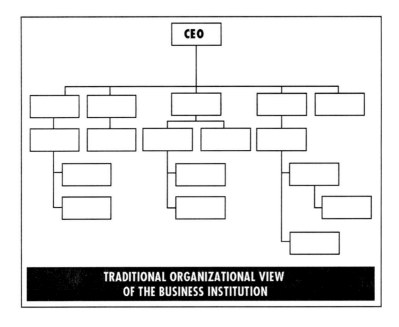

Having authority flow for all decisions only through the organizational structure, especially in large organizations, creates too many levels for rapid decision making. Management gurus have tried to improve the speed of making decisions by flattening the organizations, believing that increasing the span of reporting makes the organization more agile and decision-driven, but that hasn't happened.

RoundTable and BusinessLoop create agility in a different way by having authority flow based on the type of decision to be made—not based on who reports to whom on the organization chart.

There are three broad categories of decisions:

1. Personnel decisions: care and feeding of participants, their review against performance standards for their stated contributions and their expectations, and their compensation;

2. Functional decisions: functional competencies, standards, and skills required to accomplish a functional aspect of the business institution's work flow, and

3. Cross-functional decisions: those that flow across and through multiple functional levels *and layers* of the organizational structure.

CEO MOMENT #11
The more a business institution is focused toward long-term sustainability, the greater number of cross-functional decisions there will be.

CEO MOMENT

For people and functional decisions, it is appropriate in every organization to have authority flow through the organizational structure. In either environment, the organization chart continues to reflect the appropriate reporting structure inside the functions.

Functional managers continue to be responsible for training, reviewing, and rewarding of their direct reports and for holding the output of the function to a committed standard. People want to know how they fit into the organization and who they should look to for personal concerns, such as training or compensation. Organizational structure appropriately answers this need.

However, when you try to force cross-functional decisions for issues and opportunities to follow the organizational chart, you are clinging to the old belief of control and resisting the true belief that no one person or set of persons can ever see the whole. The company loses the impact of a larger framing and misses the inclusion of diversity of thought and experience.

With BusinessLoop and RoundTable methodologies, the authority to make cross-functional decisions flows non-hierarchically instead of following a pre-defined path through the fixed lines of reporting relationships of the organization chart.

This does not dispute that every business institution needs to have an orderly and formal organizational structure. The organization chart expresses the authority flow for personnel and functional decisions. However, it is counterproductive to use the organization chart to define the flow of authority for cross-functional decisions.

The Three Systems: Work Systems

Work Systems is the coordinated activity that participants perform to build a product or deliver a service. This activity occurs either within a function or cross-functionally. When activities are truly functional, work systems decision making follows the flow of the organization chart. With highly skilled and motivated functional experts, magic can and does happen within the functional boxes. The CEO cannot lose sight of this.

However, the more products and services a company provides, the more there is a need for cross-functional coordination and collaboration of work-systems decisions. As the need for all participants to consider more of the whole increases, functional experts who haven't accepted the new beliefs are inclined to focus even more on their functional activities. In the past, that is how they have been rewarded personally and financially.

BusinessLoops help functional managers recognize, accept, create, and protect a work-flow environment that allows their direct reports to participate in making cross-functional business decisions without requiring line approval, as long as those decisions are made by following the RoundTable and BusinessLoop methodologies.

The Three Systems: Communications Systems

Every business needs communications and information between people to carry out activities. It is impossible to live in this age of data and information without being hyper-aware that *Communications Systems* drive our businesses. We have computers full of so much functional, market, and technical information that it is easy to lose sight that every business's sustainability is based on acquiring specific customers who have specific needs and desires and the ability to pay for having those needs and desires satisfied. Sustainability is based on our success with customers as reflected in the P&L, not on how much data we have or how much we "communicate."

Communication and the understanding of data improve when participants use both words and pictures. BusinessLoop and RoundTable are the tools to match and communicate the data and information that supports the work activities and to set aside data that is not relevant or is distracting. The RoundTable tools of *dialogue not debate* and *content and envelope* improve the movement of communications.

Well-intended participants may know how things are supposed to work, but until they have a shared understanding of their activity within the flow of the entire business, they cannot take into account and appreciate all the true effects that their decisions and actions can have on customer transactions.

Example of a simple Business Flow

A Business Flow map is not static. It is the established baseline to understand how revised or new activities will affect the business. Business Flow takes things participants in the company already know and puts them together in a different way. It gives all participants the opportunity to better forecast the potential financial impact of every day-by-day decision on long-term sustainability as well as on short-term performance.

There is no one correct way to draw a Business Flow. Use any diagram that is meaningful to your company as long as it acknowledges the three environments in which your business's participants exist:

- **Environment A:** Employees and their activities,

- **Environment B:** Suppliers and business partners, and

- **Environment C:** Customers along with the influences of community, government, and competition.

Let's pretend that we start a business together making a single product—black coat hangers. You are the expert at bending wire and I have the relationships with the neighborhood dry cleaners. Our company, Bend & Send Wire Hangers, is unique and has an edge on our competitors because we make black coat hangers that we can deliver in two days, while other companies take five days to get their black coat hangers out the door.

We only have two people who perform activities and need to communicate: you and me. I handle the selling and the administration. You handle the product, shipping, and suppliers. We secure our first order. With a single customer, a single supplier, and a single product, the mapping of our Business Flow is simple.

Figure 5.3: Bend & Send's Business Flow – one product, one supplier, and one customer

The mapping of our Business Flow is about as simple and linear as you can get. However, every human participant in Bend & Send is affected by the choices and behavior of every other participant, which means that this process picture does not reflect the impact of human choice.

Complexity picks up as we add new customers and then increases even more as Bend & Send hires additional employees to keep up with our growth. What made sense to communicate by word of mouth when there were only two of us, now requires documentation because we have thirty people (a lot of them our relatives) working in the factory, answering phones, and driving our delivery trucks. One of those thirty people is my Uncle Jerry who processes orders.

Let's say our coat hanger business now gets a new customer who doesn't care so much about two-day delivery but wants five-hundred, pink coat hangers for a charity event that will be held in five weeks.

I like the idea of orders that we can schedule further out than forty-eight hours and happily write up the order for pink hangers emailing it to my Uncle Jerry to review and feed into manufacturing. I also see the marketing potential of colorful hangers and start thinking about how we might go about expanding our product line based on additional colors.

Uncle Jerry receives the order and recognizes that the customer wants a lighter color than black. He knows that pink is a custom color and that it will take at least three weeks to get it from our supplier. Uncle Jerry believes that our competitive advantage of two-day delivery is more important to all customers than a specific color; hangers get covered up by clothes after all.

Well-intended, he decides to change the order to white hangers without telling anyone. White is a stock color available with twenty-four-hour delivery and (in my uncle's mind at least) close enough to pink.

Uncle Jerry ignored the authority flow defined by the organizational structure. He changed the work flow from black to white hangers and changed the customer's order from pink to white hangers. He did all this without communicating any of his actions to the other internal participants, let alone to the customer.

Uncle Jerry just executed a Business Flow for coat hangers, but it wasn't the Business Flow for our pink coat hanger customer. We are going to end up with five-hundred white hangers that no one ordered and a potentially dissatisfied customer who wanted pink.

Thousands of hours and millions of dollars have been invested in organizational consultants, process control gurus, and information technology experts without successfully finding a way to have organizational structure, work systems, and communications systems function seamlessly together. This is where the Relationship Flow enters in.

The Relationship Flow component of the BusinessLoop tool

The problem is that most management tools treat these three networked systems as being independent and do not map out or even recognize the constant interaction that occurs at the human interfaces of the participants.

They largely ignore or try to eliminate the variability of human behavior. Human behavior isn't easily predicted or mapped, but minimizing or factoring out human variability doesn't make it go away or make its influence any less real. Instead we need to use consistent methodology to factor it *in*.

Human variability is why the linkage of the RoundTable process for collaboration is a prerequisite for the successful coordination of all business activity.

We aren't going to be successful in trying to linearly map the variability of human behavior. What we are going to do is use the additional metaphor of Relationship Flow, which is every bit as real as organizational structure, work systems, and communications systems but is non-linear.

For the CEO to build an enduring flow of trusting relationships with all the participants involved in his Business Flow requires taking the intuitive, right-brain, RoundTable Methodology and applying it to all of the human interfaces in the Business Flow. It begins with his employees inside the institution working within the three Business Flow networks and then to the two outside environments (Figure 5.1).

Whatever your Business Flow looks like, the Relationship Flow of your participants is real and needs to be managed through the Round-Table methodology. The Relationship Flow (Figure 5.4) ties all internal and external participants to the customer through activity instead of the reporting hierarchy of the organization chart. It shows how individuals are aligned to contribute to the CEO's vision from their expertise and responsibility as parts of the whole rather than as separate functional silos. This will tie the company to its customers as the participants deliver on their commitments to carry out the CEO's vision.

Relationship Flow shows as a wavy line that flows through the three systems and three environments of the business and represents the human relationships of all the participants.

Figure 5.4: The Relationship Flow

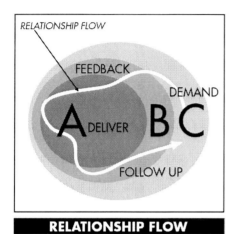

- **Environment A:** Employees and their activities,

- **Environment B:** Suppliers and business partners, and

- **Environment C:** Customers and the influences of community, government, and competition.

Relationship Flow is established based on the issue or opportunity the RoundTable is addressing. It is not random or static and is comprised of people inside and outside the business organization structure who are impacted by addressing the problem or opportunity.

CEO MOMENT #12
Apply the tools of RoundTable and BusinessLoop together in your own environment to understand the impact of relationship flow enough to build your own BusinessLoop.

Through the Relationship Flow developed by applying the Round-Table methodology, the CEO wants all the business institution's relationships to be maintained consistent with his vision for long-term sustainability.

Let's apply Relationship Flow to the Bend & Send Business Flow example. Our coat hanger business needs a stated process that takes into account the enduring reality of human variability (in this case Uncle Jerry's), while being flexible enough to change and adapt to the needs of new customers who might want pink or any other color. Bend & Send may have looked to Uncle Jerry like a straight linear connection, as in Figure 5.3, but Figure 5.5 shows the non-linear reality represented by the wavy line of the Relationship Flow.

"My nephew should give me a raise for finding out what didn't work."

— Uncle Jerry

When Bend & Send was producing only black coat hangers the relationship ribbon provided a direct line of site from the participants to the customer. After the company hires Uncle Jerry and more employees, signs up multiple customers, and adds pink hangers to the product line, that linear relationship of Business Flow has the wavy line of human variability added to it.

Figure 5.5: Bend & Send's BusinessLoop—two products, two suppliers, and two customers—and the evolving to a flow of relationship.

The Bend & Send example illustrates a company expanding from the simplest Business Flow of a single product for a single customer to the added complexity of multiple customers. Whether a company maps every Relationship Flow or not, those individual flows exist for each customer.

Relationship Flow overlays whatever Business Flow you are going to put into effect. Just as organizational structure, work flow, and communications flow are very real and linear, Relationship Flow is very real but non-linear. The Relationship Flow defines itself by the relationships of people to people at the interfaces and needs to be managed through the RoundTable methodology. This Relationship Flow is as solid as the three networks. When people cannot see how a problem exists in their Business Flow networks it probably is happening in the Relationship Flow.

In the beginning, as the CEO leads the participants in learning the RoundTable and Business Loop tools, he will almost always begin with a RoundTable issue that "seems" to reside in one of the three systems in his Business Flow.

By taking into consideration the human influences in making and implementing decisions, the Relationship Flow process will begin to ground the participants in the understanding of the interplay between the organizational structure, work systems, and communications systems. They will illuminate the granularity and constant interactivity of people, process, and procedure. Even in very large business environments where there is so much customer detail that it must be aggregated by market, someone in the company or representing the company has the individual relationship with the customer.

Relationship Flows are not static and change constantly as the needs and desires of the customers change and as internal and external participants move in and out of the business or change their behavior. The CEO wants all customer relationships handled in the name of the business institution and consistent with his vision.

CEO MOMENT #13
The CEO wants to know that someone in the institution is accountable and responsible for managing trusting relationships with customers and all other external participants in keeping with the CEO's vision.

CEO MOMENT

Figure 5.6A shows the simplest BusinessLoop possible—a company with one product, one supplier, and one customer has a single customer Relationship Flow.

Figure 5.6A: The Simple BusinessLoop is the Relationship Flow over the Business Flow

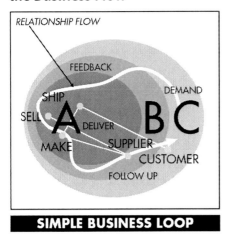

- **Environment A:** Employees and their activities,

- **Environment B:** Suppliers and business partners, and

- **Environment C:** Customers and the influences of community, government, and competition.

Figure 5.6B shows a BusinessLoop in a complex business environment. In a complex environment with many products, customers, business partners, and suppliers, it is easy to lose sight of how daily functional activities influence the Relationship Flow for any one particular customer. Whether the company and its BusinessLoops are simple or complex, the Relationship Flow works the same way for both. Decisions support the relationship first, not the functional measurements.

Figure 5.6B: The complex BusinessLoop

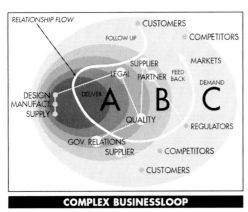

- **Environment A:** Employees and their activities,

- **Environment B:** Suppliers and business partners, and

- **Environment C:** Customers and the influences of community, government, and competition.

The CEO overlays the Business Flow with the Relationship Flow to create a powerful driver for implementing his vision of institutional long-term sustainability. He has created the broadest frame possible for including all the influences that need to be taken into consideration in the short-term for his institution's long-term sustainability. He has created a BusinessLoop that encircles all of the business's participants as they contribute to the CEO's vision for long-term sustainability.

All participants, internal and external, see how the CEO prioritizes and focuses the business's assets to understand, build, and maintain the trusting relationships that are the foundation for the long-term sustainability of his business. Participants trust the CEO to hold the largest frame possible to see the influences that they can't see in prioritization and decision making for executing his vision for the future. And the CEO trusts the participants to handle the detail and resolve issues experienced in the Business Flow at the interfaces where he cannot be.

BusinessLoop for looking to the future vision

The CEO and the business institution have short-term issues and long-term desires. BusinessLoops provide a way for the rest of the company to map into the CEO's vision in the short-term while thinking about the potential affect on the long-term health of the business. In some cases, the CEO may want to choose short-term actions that move toward the desired future vision. In other cases, the CEO will want to ensure that the short-term actions chosen do not preclude the company from reaching the vision for long-term sustainability.

When consistently implemented, the BusinessLoop provides the tool that the CEO and board of directors will use to see what is not currently running as smoothly as they would like and also to see the roadmap to the future. The BusinessLoop for your company will be the detail you will need behind the representation in Figure 5.6B.

Scenario planning is an excellent tool for helping participants hypothesize about future possibilities. But there is a gap between envisioning future possibilities and being able to use that information in the present for short-term decision making and resource allocation. The BusinessLoop, by providing a map of all current activities in an organization, can bridge that gap.

For example, participants can anticipate that their market doesn't want a product or service any longer by constantly monitoring customer relationships through BusinessLoop. This BusinessLoop-based thinking uncovers the options for expanding the future product/market segments before the anticipated "end of the life" of the current product/market segments. What actions can be taken if there is a high probability demand will ebb? How can participants change what they are doing in the short-term to accommodate this possibility? What if a part of the business recognizes the issue and the rest of the participants cannot see it at all?

The conclusion might be that a particular product or customer relationship has reached the end of its DNA. If that is the case, use the BusinessLoop to create a plan to manage that product or relationship to the end of its life cycle and be prepared to shift resources accordingly. The only other option is to wait until customers stop buying the company's products and write off the inventory. The VCR industry met its demise because of a shift in media technology not because of quality problems with VCRs.

No business process will ever reach a perfect stop point because of the variability of the environment and human participants, and because no one can ever see the whole. The purpose is to gather and share as much knowledge as possible through the RoundTable process in the time allotted. This is completed at such a level that directionally correct decisions can be made, knowing they are not perfect. If an alternative is not going to yield, it is better to act accordingly and share it with all participants so they can see what does not work and then try a different approach sooner.

In this context the BusinessLoop is effective for introducing a new product or service as well as fixing something that is broken. The CEO can look at the effect of an acquisition or a new product/market segment and assess how those decisions would affect the business. How would the new BusinessLoop layer in additional revenue and cost? What would be the synergistic and/or incremental functional activity?

The goal is not for perfection by seeing every alternative and picking the perfect one. Perfection is not a realizable or appropriate goal, not even if we do the best we can at collaboration and have the best tools for coordination. Since we can never know the whole, there is always the possibility of unknown conditions that will preclude or inhibit the results we desire.

A point to underscore is that, even in making an imperfect decision, we evaluate people on their functional performance. All participants are still accountable for making choices, executing their activity to their functional standards, and delivering on their commitments.

CEO REFLECTIONS

- What percent of budgets and resources will you commit to creating and monitoring a frame that includes all of your customers plus all of your participants?

- What is your reaction to the three systems and wanting authority to flow differently based on whether the decision is functional or cross-functional?

- Are you satisfied that decisions are made quickly and with agility?

- How do authority and resources flow to make and implement decisions in your organization?

- How does the company monitor progress on decisions and make adjustments if necessary?

Chapter 6

BusinessLoop Examples

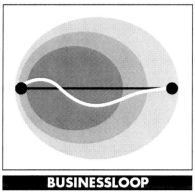

BUSINESSLOOP

For Coordination

When a business institution does have problems, how do participants prioritize what to address first? How do they know that in fixing one problem, they don't cause more problems at other points?

BusinessLoops provide a way of framing all issues so that the CEO and other participants are able to follow them and prioritize them while recognizing that they don't control the environment and no one person can see the whole. BusinessLoops give a framework for quick reaction to problems as they occur. The RoundTable and BusinessLoop tools operate together to create an evolving picture that encourages continuous dialogue, rather than a passive snapshot that sits on the shelf in a binder.

This framing helps participants integrate other sources of information about the business that may be acquired from articles, books, and consultants. BusinessLoop is a tool for seeing more of the total environment and making better, more informed decisions by identifying and then including the people affected. But this by itself does not guarantee that the CEO or participants can ever see the whole and, thereby, make perfect decisions. It does not guarantee that all RoundTable participants will honor their commitments to the Table.

As you begin to consider how you might structure a Business-Loop in your environment, think in terms of the three systems. Is the issue you would like to resolve showing itself in the organization structure, the work systems, or the communications systems? Thinking back to the three environments explained in Chapter 5 (Figure 5.6A), which internal and external participants are affected?

Figure 5.6A: The Simple BusinessLoop is the Relationship Flow over the Business Flow

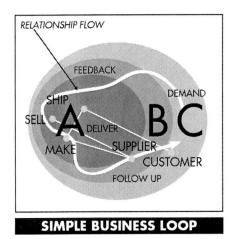

- **Environment A:** Employees and their activities,

- **Environment B:** Suppliers and business partners, and

- **Environment C:** Customers and the influences of community, government, and competition.

ESGO: "Teamwork makes the dream work." An "Environment A" example

This case illustrates how relationships built only on the desirable attributes of friendship and loyalty among employees can get in the way of appropriate authority flow to the detriment of the long-term sustainability of the business institution. The RoundTable and BusinessLoop tools can be used to bring relationship activity back into alignment and correct any misuse of authority.

At Express Signs & Graphics of Orlando (ESGO), the business issue at first looked like a communications issue between production and sales. Eric, the owner of ESGO, used "Teamwork makes the dream work" as a slogan at a company meeting to reflect his desire to found a business built on respectful and beneficial relationships with his employees, business partners, and customers.

Because he personally was very good at customer contact and customer care, and had the desire to be a quality supplier, Eric believed that the people he employed would automatically line up and do their best just because they were part of the team. His friend Joe, a salesperson who had a good way of meeting and connecting with people through group contacts, agreed to join him to get the business going.

The sign business is specific to each customer. The colors, type fonts, graphics, and layout for each order are often unique. Like the simple Business Flow of Bend & Send with only black coat hangers, as long as ESGO was comprised of Eric, the graphic designer, and Joe, Eric could keep watch over what was going on. He had the view from the customer through design, into production, and then out through shipping and install.

The business grew and Eric added people. Eric operated as if everyone was as committed to the long-term sustainability of ESGO as he was.

However, participants, being human, did not always carry out their commitments. There would always be a "reason" why something wasn't done according to what was agreed. The results were more cost, late or delayed orders, and customer dissatisfaction.

ESGO undertakes RoundTable and BusinessLoop

When having a happy, harmonious team did not preclude his business from having a problem receiving and processing orders, Eric undertook the Business Flow.

RELATIONSHIP FLOW

	SALES & MARKETING	GRAPHIC DESIGN	PRODUCTION	DELIVERY & INSTALLATIONS	BILLING & COLLECTIONS	CUSTOMER SATISFACTION
STRATEGIES	• DIRECT SALES • NETWORKING • MARKET FOCUS	• BEST DESIGN SKILLS • INCREASE CAPACITY • DECREASE ERRORS	• REDUCE WASTE • INCREASE CAPACITY • IMPROVE QUALITY	• SUB OUT ALL INSTALLS • USE BEST SUBCONTRACTORS • GET BEST PRICES FROM SUBS	• GET $$$ FASTER • GET $$$ EASIER	• BEST SIGN QUALITY • MEET DEADLINES • MEASURE CUSTOMERS' SATISFACTION • KEEP CUSTOMERS UP-DATED ON ORDER STATUS
ISSUES	• LEAD GENERATION • RECRUITING REPS • PROFITABLE JOBS	• DEPT. DESIGN SKILLS • DEPT. CAPACITY/CYCLE • FINDING NETWORK FILES	• INVENTORY MANAGEMENT • MATERIAL STORAGE SPACE • CAPACITY	• INSURANCE COST & RISKS • NOT ENOUGH DETAIL ON SCOPE OF INSTALLS	• CASH FLOW WEAK • TIME CONSUMING • INVOICES NOT DESCRIPTIVE	• FAST ORDER STATUS • MOTIVATE ESGO TO BE CUSTOMER SERVICE AWARE • GET PRICING OUT FAST
GOALS & ACTIVITIES	• INCREASE SALES 2.5% • HIRE MORE REPS • NEW COMMISISION PLAN	• STANDARD PDF PROOF • TRAIN/HIRE PERSONNEL • NEW FILE NAMING SYSTEM	• RESEARCH FLAG MATERIAL • INCREASE COLOR MANAGEMENT • CREATE PROFILE LIBRARY	• GETTING SUB-CONTRACTOR QUOTES BEFORE QUOTING • KEEP INSURANCE	• STANDARDIZE QUOTES • STANDARDIZE INVOICES • TOUGHER STANDARDS FOR EXTENDING CREDIT	• SALES REPS TO KEEP OFFICE HOURS • MONTHLY THANK YOU NOTES

FIGURE 6.1: ESGO BUSINESSLOOP – "ENVIRONMENT A" EXAMPLE

The ESGO Business Flow map was a basic chart from customer to order write-up into production, shipment, and collections (Figure 6.1). Using those as broad headings, Eric captured the problems, strategies, issues, and needs of ESGO. This showed which participants needed to perform which activities for a given product to be delivered, accepted, and paid for by the customer. Solid arrows between and under each function show the linear left brain to-dos that would be in the three networks.

Eric understood the BusinessLoop graphic and appreciated the focus it brought. Once he defined, in block form, all the participants by function and what they did to create the product and deliver it to the end-user, he was ready to bring in his employees using the RoundTable process.

He used the RoundTable process to map the Relationship Flow overlaying the functions required to receive, produce, and deliver customer orders. The wavy line of Relationship Flow represents the people connections being non-linear and needing the Round-Table methodology and tools. Using the Business Flow pictures, Eric convened a RoundTable to deal with quality and cost in booking and entering orders.

The participants at the order processing RoundTable represented the functions of design, production, and sales. I served as his facilitator. We used an existing order for grocery store banners as a framework for our discussion for ESGO to establish an ongoing order processing Roundtable to address the quality and cost issues. The agreed-to process was that all quotations would come to the order processing RoundTable for review and assessment against agreed-upon conditions before being given to the customer.

If the quotation followed the RoundTable process for order review, met the conditions for acceptance, and was then accepted by the customer, the order could be scheduled for production. If either the process or the order conditions were not met, the order processing RoundTable had Eric's authority to refuse to accept the order for production. However, they were to continue to dialogue on what could be done to make it an acceptable order, not just reject it.

Authority flow of the organizational structure is tested

Although Eric's issue appeared as a problem in the communications and functional systems of his Business Flow, things turned out to be quite different. The root of ESGO's problem was in the organizational structure and flow of authority. The functional teams knew how to design and produce signs. The salespeople knew the correct way to write orders. There was a good process defined. The problem was that one of the sales people chose to override it.

Eric delegated the authority to approve orders to the Round-Table, not to the sales people. His friend, Joe, started to override the RoundTable and went directly to production with his orders because of what he thought were "urgent" customer needs. The people in production, who knew the relationship between Eric and Joe, assumed that Joe must have Eric's agreement to ignore the process, so they produced and shipped the orders as Joe wrote them.

More often than not, these orders contained errors that would have been identified and corrected had Joe followed the RoundTable process. Since he didn't, his orders usually shipped with errors. This caused accounts receivable problems, rework, and deeply discounted concessions because the customer couldn't or wouldn't pay.

Eric was frustrated. He had started his business to get away from similar problems in the large company environment. As he was trying to bring harmony and quality to his work and communications systems, his authority flow was being tested. It is important to underscore a distinction here. It wasn't a hierarchical reporting structure that was being subverted. It was the decision-making process as defined by the order processing RoundTable that was bypassed.

The situation was costing Eric margin and was going against the one thing he was hoping to have—a wonderful culture of shared goals and teamwork to reach them. Instead, the Relationship Flow of the human systems and the Business Flow of the communications and work systems were being driven apart.

For reasons that he thought were good, Joe went against the agreed upon, decision-making process and usurped authority that he didn't have. The rest of the ESGO participants thought that Eric condoned it. The participants needed to see the ramifications of not following the flow of authority for the decisions made at the RoundTable.

CEO MOMENT #14
To be responsible for the long-term sustainability of the business, CEOs must enforce business processes and risk damaging personal relationships temporarily.

CEO MOMENT

This is hard to do, and never harder than when influential relationships or friendships are involved. BusinessLoops can provide an unemotional framework for dealing with these types of influences by observing the facts and total effects in the real world.

Eric began to sit in on the order-processing Table, supplying the CEO's discipline to the Business Flow when decisions were made. He re-established the integrity of the RoundTable and Business Flow processes requiring Joe to adhere to the process and restoring trust between the participants. The team benefited. Joe saw how his well-intended sense of urgency could be detrimental both to his customer and the company.

Human variability overrides solid process

How many times do we see similar examples in large corporations as CEOs and senior leaders make exceptions and compromise the agreed-upon process? The bigger the business, the more the example of Eric's learned experience rings true, even when CEOs are well intended. Just telling people the right thing to do and having all the processes in place for authority, work systems, and communications systems does not guarantee the desired result, especially if exceptions are arbitrarily practiced.

As long as participants have choice, those with authority or assumed authority can override the system. It is up to the CEO to create an environment where this is not acceptable behavior; there must be serious consequences when someone makes an exception without exposing it to the light of day.

This is the tough part of this model. Some CEOs will want to retain the latitude to do something for their own self-interest. They express this by saying that the CEO needs the flexibility to make exceptions. If valid reasons for an exception to any process are discovered, then the process needs to be re-evaluated with the new information. If one exception is allowed without changing the process, then the process is not solid or the CEO's commitment to his stated beliefs is not solid.

ARDIS: A first-generation wireless data network. An "Environment B" example

In Chapter 3 we introduced ARDIS, the wireless data company, where we further developed the RoundTable methodology. In this case study, ARDIS highlights the use of BusinessLoop to address issues in the "B Environment" with business partners and suppliers. Just as in ESGO, ARDIS needed to resolve the issues related to Business Flow and Relationship Flow between employees inside the company "A Environment" before doing so with the external environments.

At ARDIS, we used the terminology *Business Flow Solution* to describe the interaction of work, communications, and organizational structure among internal and external participants. There was an excellent understanding of data flow; after all, the business was a wireless data network. However, when it came to work flow, there was no appreciation of the linkages between the business functions.

There was little recognition or willingness to understand that the participants were missing their commitments to the P&L because of the lack of collaboration and coordination between the functions. When issues arose, the functional silos would not acknowledge that they had need of the input from other functions or admit that their decisions and output affected others. Our facilitator, Janet P., led us through the group construct of a high-level Business Flow of an ARDIS' BusinessLoop.

As a network operator, ARDIS needed viable device suppliers, applications providers, and software providers to connect the device to the customers' legacy computer applications systems. We were relying on other businesses, silos if you will, to help us satisfy our customers.

It became clear that to succeed, ARDIS needed to develop more than an arm's distance supplier relationship with these entities. We needed them to become true business partners who, without being obligated legally, would work in collaboration and coordination with us to satisfy our mutual customers' needs. Before we could develop a trusting Relationship Flow with outside participants we needed to have a trusting relationship flow between our internal functions.

As these relationships were brought to life on a BusinessLoop map (Figure 6.2), the functional leaders scrutinized the critical linkages required at the interfaces between ARDIS and our suppliers and business partners to produce the end product that the customer was buying.

Their appreciation increased for the activities and functions being performed by the external business partners and their awareness grew for how internal and external activities needed to link together for our success. ARDIS employees began to understand that what was true for the outside linkages with business partners was also true for the function-to-function linkages inside ARDIS.

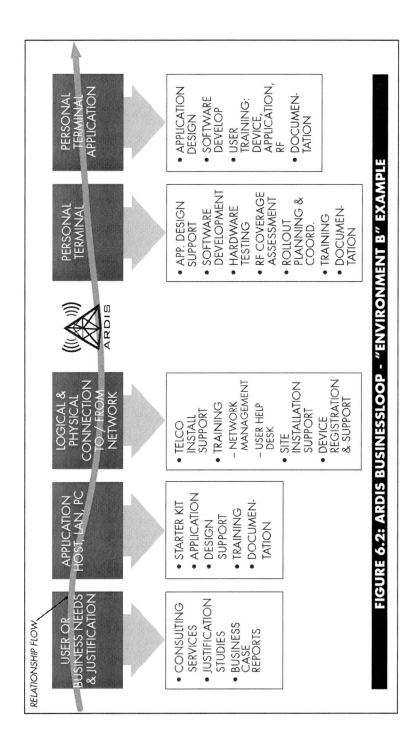

FIGURE 6.2: ARDIS BUSINESSLOOP - "ENVIRONMENT B" EXAMPLE

The network operator was at the end of the food chain. We didn't get paid until the customer was satisfied with the device and the application, and was using the network. Therefore, we ended up taking the lead in fostering cooperative and collaborative relationships among the multiple suppliers and business partners, not by desire but by necessity. Even though we did not manufacture the device or application, we were held accountable for the experience the customer was perceiving—just like AT&T and Verizon are held accountable (at least initially) for problems with smart phone applications.

ARDIS had the same complexity internally that ESGO had, only compounded. Although ARDIS had issues in authority and communications systems, our biggest challenges occurred in the work flow systems that tied us with our business partners. The customers looked to us to resolve issues that were in another business partner's domain because it was our invoice as the network operator that the customers saw monthly.

At one point we were contacted by the owner of a device manufacturer to help resolve a customer issue. He was upset because he wasn't getting paid for his hardware and there was finger pointing between our organizations. Although the devices were operational, the customer could not use them because the application was not operating properly. It was not the device or the network. We were missing a key participant, the applications provider, whose behavior was affecting our collective Business Flow.

We approached this third business partner with our arms open and all our cards on the table. Nothing was hidden. We used the Business Flow chart to identify what was known and what was unknown about the problem. We talked about the connections and ways that we could fit together to deliver the value-add of one-plus-one-plus-one. The device manufacturer said, "Wow. I never looked at our relationship this way before."

After this experience, I realized that we could use this picture of the Business Flow for problem solving, relationship planning, and market focus by evaluating all of the relationships between the market players to knit the three systems internally and externally with business partners and customers.

Eventually we used these Business Flow diagrams and charts to bring all of the internal and external participants together to see what was happening inside this chain of relationships that the customer viewed as one. It wasn't to deflect responsibility or accountability. It was to demonstrate the reality of the co-dependencies. As we brought this perspective to our external business partners, they began to see everyone's unique expertise as well as the critical need to participate with us in managing the external linkages that created the foundation of the customer's overall experience. The recognition of our shared reality with our business partners gave us the tool that began to turn the business around.

The North and South Americas pricing RoundTable breaks down. An "Environment C" example

This last case study returns to the Motorola pricing RoundTable example discussed in Chapter 4. This experience illuminates the broadness of BusinessLoop by adding to the complexity of ESGO and ARDIS. In this example, we are dealing with multiple customers in multiple countries plus the additional external influences of community, government, and competition.

Figure 6.3 illustrates North and South America's BusinessLoop for use in pricing and forecasting profit and loss. It shows the internal and external complexity with the Relationship Flow weaving through both.

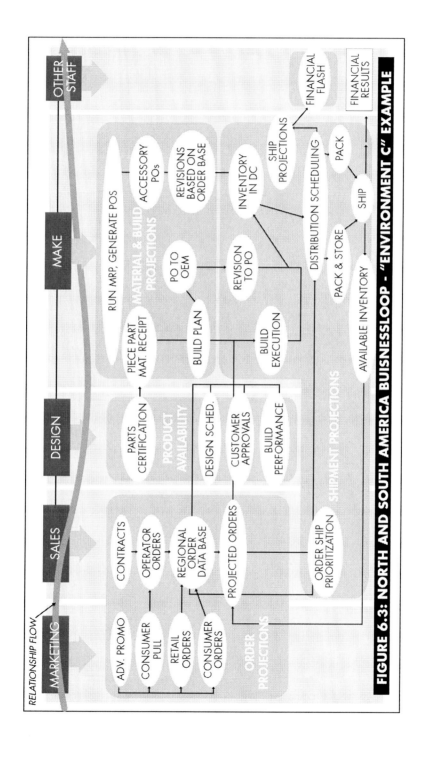

FIGURE 6.3: NORTH AND SOUTH AMERICA BUISNESSLOOP - "ENVIRONMENT C" EXAMPLE

In only a couple of months, the RoundTable process on pricing became so ingrained with the North and South American country managers that the participants were operating together on other issues. The Business Flow tool was being used appropriately to keep all pricing participants aware of changes (whether from new issues or new opportunities) so that they could assess and feedback through the pricing RoundTable the impact of those changes to their country operations, the shared staff, and the CEO's business as a whole.

I had supplied the discipline to put the RoundTable process in place and get it operating, but I didn't bring new or more relevant input to the dialog on current pricing issues. The group had needed me for envelope, but when it came to content, it was the people in operational roles who contributed the expertise.

With the RoundTable being consistently implemented by using the BusinessLoop process reflected in Figure 6.3, my direct participation was no longer required at this table. That is until a very large Canadian network operator put in an order for new cellular phones. As valuable as RoundTabling can be, no tool in the world will preclude human beings from making choices that aren't in the best interest of the whole. The pricing RoundTable "chose" a course of action that we all agreed to follow but, as we were to discover the hard way, we could not "control" its execution as a member of the Table "chose" to act on his own. Here's what happened.

The Canadian country manager brought this order to the pricing RoundTable. This order would put Motorola on the map in Canada, a market that was especially impacted by pricing and cross-border shipments. The participants discussed it and came to a price that the country manager of Canada agreed to, although reluctantly.

He left the table and called me to see if he could get a lower price by circumventing the RoundTable decision. I brought him back to the Table and asked the group to review once more the numbers and the impact. What he wanted to do was not in the best interest of Motorola, so the RoundTable pricing held.

Within a couple of days of the announcement of the new product, a huge new order from Canada came in. My office was quickly filled with U.S. people and my finance executive telling me that we had to fire the Canadian country manager. They had heard from their customers—the U.S. carriers—that we had given a Canadian customer a lower price than the U.S. price. The Canadian operator took advantage of this lower price by purchasing more product than they needed for their own network loading. They subsidized their own business revenue by reselling this additional product back into the U.S.; the customer was engaging in arbitrage.

I listened and said I couldn't believe it. The Canadian manager had committed to me and to the pricing RoundTable that he wouldn't do this. The U.S. managers and the CFO were ready to shoot him, but I insisted that there must be some other facts that we did not know. I called the Canadian manager to a meeting of the pricing RoundTable and asked him for the additional facts. He stiffened up, pumped out his chest, and said, "I know I committed to adhering to the price we agreed to at the RoundTable, but I changed it for the good of my customer. It was the right thing to do for my customer."

I told him that I appreciated him doing what he thought was right for his customer, but did he see the impact that it was having on our company? Did he understand that he had a higher responsibility? That his first responsibility was to the company and his peers who he sat with and was committed to? If he felt so strongly that he had gone back on his agreement, he should have come back to the RoundTable to tell his associates that this was his plan.

CEO MOMENT #15
Any abuse of the RoundTable responsibility must be openly addressed by the CEO.

CEO MOMENT

"I thought that you would talk me out of it," he said. "We would have," I told him. "This is a $2.5 million swing to the bottom line profit for the company. Knowing that your customer would go against his agreement with you and cross-border ship, would you do this again?"

His shoulders dropped, and he agreed that he had done the wrong thing by agreeing to one price and then going against his word. "You are going to fire me, aren't you?" he asked.

It is the CEO's responsibility to ensure that the RoundTable and BusinessLoop tools are applied with consistency. The appropriate addressing of any abuse of RoundTable responsibility may be to release the offending participant from his job, or there may be a greater gain to the total organization by using his example to underscore the RoundTable and BusinessLoop process. Either way, the CEO must openly and overtly deal with the situation.

Human variability can cause some participants' behavior to override even the best systems and processes. However, if the person is well-intended, you may still gain from it.

In this case, firing the Canadian manager would have been easy. He had broken the trust of the RoundTable. The institution's asset of trust was compromised. But firing is not always the best way to teach the tools of RoundTable and BusinessLoop. This manager had made a serious mistake, but it was with good intentions for his customer. If he had been ill-intended I would have fired him on the spot.

"I'm not going to fire you," I told him. "I just spent $2.5 million for your education. You are going to be my poster boy for the integrity of the RoundTable process." It was a very expensive tuition, but he became a RoundTable zealot. The story took on legend status, which became a huge driver in expediting the acceptance of this way of managing and leading, and it reinforced for me that even in the worst situation, if the person is well-intended, you can learn from it. We also learned that not all orders are good orders for the institution.

When I didn't take the Canadian manager out, the rest of the organization (even though they wanted him fired) recognized two things more completely than they had before: that I had compassion and understanding of just how difficult it can be for deeply held old beliefs to be changed, and that I was willing to give authority to the RoundTable so completely that such authority could be abused. They now *really* understood that this new way of operating was not hub-and-spoke management under a different name. The experience also pointed out that another checkpoint for pricing was needed in the Business Flow, so we implemented that in-country finance would be charged with signing off on pricing for any new orders.

By assembling appropriate processes and by accepting that change is a constant by-product of all human behavior, an institution's BusinessLoop forces participants to view more of the whole and create a picture that makes it difficult for participants to ignore that any subset of the business has the potential to impact the rest of the whole.

As the people on the top deck of the Titanic tragically realized, the gash below in the ship's hull did eventually affect them, too.

It also reinforced that even the best systems and processes in the world can be overridden by humans. The RoundTable and BusinessLoop processes will work if people's behavior is well-intended; no process will totally eliminate someone's bad intentions or poor performance. In those cases, appropriate action must be taken. The new environment requires participants to deliver on their committed gives. When they don't, the CEO must take immediate action.

CEO MOMENT #16
The principles and processes of the RoundTable and BusinessLoop are the touchstone, whether the results of human variability are positive or negative.

CEO MOMENT

Human variability, whether destructive or creative, will always be present. You do not want to eliminate the possibility of unexpected behavior because often that behavior demonstrates a better way of doing things. When a person comes up with something new that impacts existing processes in a positive way, you want to change to embrace the new idea. However, when the human variability is destructive to the CEO's vision, you want to take immediate and appropriate action. Retrain, reprimand, or punish.

The RoundTable and BusinessLoop processes and principles are an agreed-upon roadmap for executing the CEO's vision for the long-term sustainability of the business institution through the balancing of the gives and gets of all the participants. These are the touchstones to determine if the effects of human variability (unexpected behavior) are destructive or constructive to executing the CEO's vision by leading from trust.

Finance and human resources are extensions of the CEO and embody the agreed-upon objectives and values of the institution.

After installing the up-front discipline and providing the training to bring RoundTable and BusinessLoop into the organization, employees are empowered to follow the process and use the tools. Eventually, many RoundTables will come and go, some permanent and some temporary; the CEO will not need to be—nor can she be—present at all of them. Recognizing the powerful impact of old beliefs on human variability, the CEO cannot leave the adherence to this new way of operating to chance. When something goes off track, especially while the organization is learning this new way of operating, the CEO wants to be alerted as quickly as possible.

If the company is large enough to have finance and human resources organizations, these functions participate in every RoundTable and BusinessLoop discussion. They provide their functional expertise and also play a larger role for the business institution as a whole. The CEO asks these two functions to be an extension of her in managing the interdependent relationship between the business institution and the participants. In this new environment, finance and human resources aren't just staff nor on the sidelines as gatekeepers, teachers, or disciplinarians. They serve as the surrogate eyes and ears of the CEO.

Human resources and finance are charged with the responsibility to ensure that information in the organization flows up and down. They help the CEO stay continuously aware of how the business institution is doing financially and how it is doing culturally without him personally having to extract all the specific detail from the RoundTables. Finance and human resources have job descriptions that cut across all functions. They are available when RoundTables ask for assistance since every action affects people and budgets.

The RoundTable participants ask finance about how their decisions and actions affect the P&L (left-brain content issues). They ask human resources to help with meeting behavior and human relationship issues (right-brain envelope issues).

Concluding the tools for trust

Just as with the RoundTable, the CEO must be an active participant in supporting BusinessLoop to change the people's old beliefs to create new behaviors. Employees may understand that the CEO wants them to take responsibility and be experimental, coordinated, and entrepreneurial, but they won't behave that way if they don't believe that the CEO will support them when something goes wrong or expected results do not materialize.

Existing managers might not want to buy into the BusinessLoop process. They will know intellectually that the business institution will benefit from this approach, but the CEO is asking them to change their beliefs and possibly give up what they perceive as ego-defining responsibility and authority. They may want a better way to have their people solve problems, but not if they have to give up their beliefs of being in control or forfeit their ego perks.

Once they begin accepting that no one knows it all, that there is no control, only choice, and, therefore, no way to program or anticipate all the possible changes, their beliefs will begin to change. They will drop the goal of perfection, use the RoundTable for rapid, inclusive decision making, and implement BusinessLoop for rapid inclusive execution. Their behavior will change.

As managers we are brought up to think there is a right and wrong answer, that there is a solution if we work harder and smarter. BusinessLoop perspective forces us to see that a business institution is a big jigsaw puzzle with missing pieces and no picture on the box; we don't have all the pieces...and we never will.

In this new environment, failure is redefined as what doesn't work. Participants release the fear of attempting something new or different because it might not succeed. They also are able to more quickly let go of activities and ideas that didn't work because they no longer have to justify ideas or activities that didn't produce the results that were anticipated.

Participants are empowered to use the CEO's authority if they adopt the values, and honor the process of the RoundTable methodology and BusinessLoop rigor for rapid decision making and implementation. They have invested the time to map for themselves their business's unique three systems of organization structure, work systems, and communications systems, agreeing to their interaction.

If any aspect from process to product is to be changed, there is the recognition that there will be multiple inputs because there will always be multiple points of interface. Evolved people who have the trust and authority from the CEO through the RoundTable and BusinessLoop can adjust activities on a real-time basis as the environment changes.

CEO MOMENT #17
Failures are part of life.
Fail as quickly as possible,
learn from it, and move on to
find the solution that works.

CEO MOMENT

The CEO wants all participants to believe that opportunities they choose are worth pursuing and that problems are worth solving. She wants every participant who can influence an opportunity or who is affected by an issue to use RoundTable and Business-Loop to address them. She wants participants' support and input for defining the issue, deciding on a course of action, implementing it, and evaluating the result.

CEO REFLECTIONS

Institutional harmony starts and takes root as RoundTabling encourages functional and personal learning. It happened between countries in Herr Braxmeir's Language, Borders, Cultures example, between functions in both the ARDIS and ESGO examples, and between both in the Motorola example.

- What similarities do you see comparing your Business-Loop to the examples of ESGO, ARDIS, and Motorola?

- Are the similarities in "Environment A, B, or C"?

- What are you experiencing as problems?

- Are these problems in the organization structure and authority, work systems, or communications systems?

- Are these problems in your Relationship Flow?

Let's go implement

In the first six chapters, we have established the uniqueness of the business institution as a standalone entity. We have defined the participant groups that influence or are influenced by the institution. In this environment, the CEO has a unique role in balancing the participant's gives and gets while carrying out her responsibility for the long-term sustainability of the business institution. We have presented RoundTable and BusinessLoop tools and processes to help the CEO and participants to perform their jobs and to ensure a consistent environment for the business institution from

CEO to CEO as the participants change out over time—all done with integrity.

The balance of the book applies the tools and thoughts of trust to make the transition away from the current environment that ferments distrust and benefits few.

Section 3

Beginning the Process of Rebuilding Trust

"Credit goes to the man who convinces the world not to the man who first has the idea."

— Sir Francis Bacon, philosopher, statesman, and scientist

Section 3 presents a pragmatic methodology for CEOs and other leaders to apply the tools of RoundTable and BusinessLoop to recreate the environment of trust.

In the current business environment of special interests, the gap of exclusion between the CEO and most of the rest of the business institution's participants has widened and created more and more distrust. Trust was not destroyed all at once but day by day because of the way priorities were set, decisions were made and implemented, and details were handled.

To successfully use the RoundTable and BusinessLoop tools to change the current environment, the CEO must complete a personal transition from the philosophy of beliefs to the pragmatics of implementation. The philosophical part of that transition is recognizing that the behavior of CEOs, and all participants' business behaviors, come from their business beliefs, which come from core values and personal beliefs. The pragmatic part is changing those personal and core beliefs to beliefs that drive the behaviors necessary to achieve the possibilities of the leadership model built on trust.

BELIEFS AND BEHAVIORS

PERSONAL BELIEFS

- WE ARE ALL CONNECTED.
- WE CANNOT SEE THE WHOLE.
- NO PARTICIPANT OR INSTITUTION LIVES FOREVER.
- NO ONE PERSON HAS CONTROL. WE HAVE ONLY CHOICE.

BUSINESS BELIEFS

- THE CEO HAS A UNIQUE RESPONSIBILITY FOR THE LONG-TERM SUSTAINABILITY OF THE BUSINESS INSTITUTION.
- EFFECTIVE SHORT-TERM DECISIONS ALWAYS CONSIDER THE LONG-TERM IMPACT.
- RELATIONSHIPS BUILT ON TRUST AND RESPECT ARE THE BASIS FOR LONG-TERM SUSTAINABILITY.
- DIVERSITY OF ALL PARTICIPANTS' PERSPECTIVES LEADS TO BETTER DECISIONS.
- THE CEO IS THE INTEGRITY COMPASS.

BUSINESS BEHAVIORS

- THE CEO HOLDS A FRAME THAT IS BROAD ENOUGH TO CONSIDER THE LONG-TERM IMPACT OF EVERY SHORT-TERM DECISION.
- PARTICPANTS DELIVER THEIR COMMITTED GIVES.
- ALL PARTICIPANTS TRUST THAT THEIR EXPECTATIONS AND VIEWS WILL BE CONSIDERED.
- THE CEO CREATES AN ENVIRONMENT FOR RAPID DECISION MAKING TO FIND OUT FASTER WHAT WORKS AND WHAT DOESN'T.
- THE CEO AND ALL PARTICIPANTS FOLLOW THE INTENT AS WELL AS THE LETTER OF THE LAW.

For most of us, especially in business, our starting point for change usually begins by looking at other people's behaviors before we look at our own. However, this change process begins with us looking at our own behaviors first.

Chapter 7

The CEO's Transition

Once CEOs define their personal transition, they then will determine the change that is necessary from other participants to move the company from the current to the desired environment.

In all areas of our personal and professional lives, our behavior is driven by what we believe, not necessarily by what is real. Whatever behavior our beliefs support, there is only one true environment. We can believe in what is true, or we can construct an alternate set of beliefs that deny or disregard some or all of reality.

Look at your own current business behaviors that you represented in CEO Exercise 1, Chapter 1. By considering the questions at the end of each previous chapter, you had your own personal reflections on the truth of your business beliefs and the business environment they create. Take another look at your self-evaluation. Is there anything you would change as you fill it out this time?

CEO Exercise 1: My Current Business Behaviors

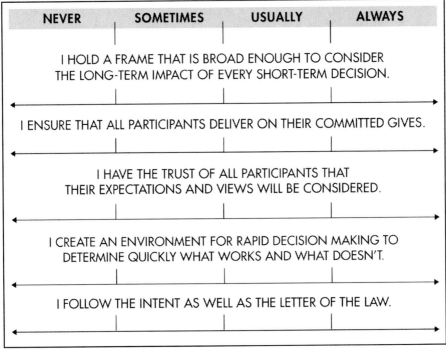

NEVER	SOMETIMES	USUALLY	ALWAYS

I HOLD A FRAME THAT IS BROAD ENOUGH TO CONSIDER THE LONG-TERM IMPACT OF EVERY SHORT-TERM DECISION.

I ENSURE THAT ALL PARTICIPANTS DELIVER ON THEIR COMMITTED GIVES.

I HAVE THE TRUST OF ALL PARTICIPANTS THAT THEIR EXPECTATIONS AND VIEWS WILL BE CONSIDERED.

I CREATE AN ENVIRONMENT FOR RAPID DECISION MAKING TO DETERMINE QUICKLY WHAT WORKS AND WHAT DOESN'T.

I FOLLOW THE INTENT AS WELL AS THE LETTER OF THE LAW.

There are CEOs whose beliefs support these behaviors and CEOs whose beliefs do not. To reach the desired environment, you and the participants in your business will want your Xes on the right-hand side of this chart. If they aren't, what are your beliefs that make it acceptable for you to NOT place your X under "always" for each one of these questions?

My transition from the old view of the environment to a new broader framing began when my European experience forced me to look at the beliefs driving my own business behavior. My reflection on where my Xes were helped me bring clarity to my business and personal beliefs as we addressed in Chapter 2.

To gain your own clarity about the business beliefs that underlie your business behavior, pick up your pencil again and, using CEO Exercise 2, place another set of Xes where you are on the continuum of *business beliefs* that support an environment of trust.

CEO Exercise 2: My Business Beliefs

DO NOT BELIEVE	WILLING TO CONSIDER	SOMEWHAT BELIEVE	BELIEVE WHOLEHEARTEDLY

THE CEO HAS THE UNIQUE RESPONSIBILITY FOR THE LONG-TERM SUSTAINABILITY OF THE BUSINESS INSTITUTION.

EFFECTIVE SHORT-TERM DECISIONS ALWAYS CONSIDER THE LONG-TERM IMPACT.

RELATIONSHIPS BUILT ON TRUST AND RESPECT ARE THE BASIS FOR LONG-TERM SUSTAINABILITY.

DIVERSITY AND INCLUSION OF ALL PARTICIPANTS' PERSPECTIVES LEAD TO BETTER DECISIONS.

THE CEO IS THE INTEGRITY COMPASS FOR THE BUSINESS INSTITUTION.

CEOs who do not share these beliefs at their core may voice support because it is difficult to publically object or disagree, but their behavior demonstrates their true beliefs. Those CEOs who feel agreement at their core with these beliefs are subjected to day-to-day pressures that, along with the way they are being paid, cause many to act counter to their core beliefs. Monthly and quarterly measurements push them toward the slippery slope of excluding the long-term ramifications of short-term decisions. If you didn't have the type of extreme pressure for short-term financial per-formance that compromises long-term sustainability, where would your Xes be?

As CEO, how would you respond to the question, "What is your number-one priority?" Investors might say shareholder value. Employees might say wages, benefits, career growth, or long-term employment. Customers might say superior product, service, or value.

Your number-one priority will drive your actions as CEO and therefore your vision. There are many CEOs who want to build a company of long-term value. These leaders disagree at their core with the pervasive top priority of short-term objectives. Is your top priority long-term sustainability of the company or is it quarterly profits and stock price? Are you telling your Board and investors one thing and the rest of the company's participants something different?

In previous pages, we looked at business behavior and you marked your self-assessment. We progressed to business beliefs and you marked where you stand on that, too. We now continue with the self-examination going one step deeper to examine how our core personal beliefs drive or influence our business beliefs.

In the exercise below, place an X where you are on the continuum of the four *personal beliefs* of the environment of trust.

CEO Exercise 3: My Personal Beliefs

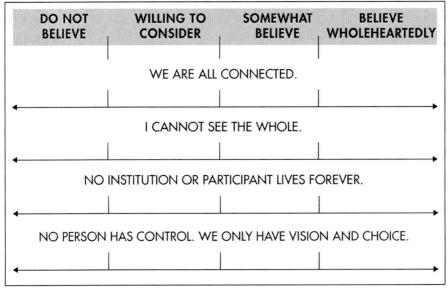

DO NOT BELIEVE	WILLING TO CONSIDER	SOMEWHAT BELIEVE	BELIEVE WHOLEHEARTEDLY

WE ARE ALL CONNECTED.

I CANNOT SEE THE WHOLE.

NO INSTITUTION OR PARTICIPANT LIVES FOREVER.

NO PERSON HAS CONTROL. WE ONLY HAVE VISION AND CHOICE.

If I had completed this exercise when I was in Europe with Herr Braxmeir, I am not sure where I would have put my marks.

Having had my experiences, CEO Moments, and Reflections, my Xes are now on the far right. I've come to understand that these are more than beliefs—they are truths.

CEOs that recognize the truths in this philosophical discussion of personal beliefs are ready to move from their current way of leading. It would be very efficient if we could change underlying beliefs by simply thinking and talking about them as we did in the early chapters of this book. But we can't.

We must recognize and then accept the logical relationship between behaviors and beliefs. Before we can ask others to participate, we need to be thoroughly grounded in these new beliefs enough to model them. We will need conviction, fortitude, tenacity, and clarity to stand up to the challenges of others inside and beyond our organizations. You will apply your own personal traits and right brain commitments to your beliefs to build the trusting relationships that allow you to get through the bumps of transition that you can't see or control.

As a lead in to mapping a plan to move toward your desired environment, we will compare the environment of benefits to few to the environment of trust that achieves long-term sustainability. Take what you've learned about yourself through the X-marking exercises, your Reflections, and your CEO Moments, and reflect on the reality of your current environment. Further reflecting in this way, you can begin moving from the philosophical vision of your ideas into your desired environment for the pragmatic implementation of them.

The frame of the environment that benefits few: Thoughts ~ Words ~ Behavior ≠ Integrity

The CEO's personal beliefs are depicted across the top in Figure 7.1. The CEO believes he is all-knowing and may even believe that he is king. He believes that his first priority is to himself. He accomplishes this priority by taking care of his board members, shareholders, and inside group. The CEO thinks he can control everything, and sees relationships with people and the environment as only a means to an end.

Figure 7.1: The environment that benefits few

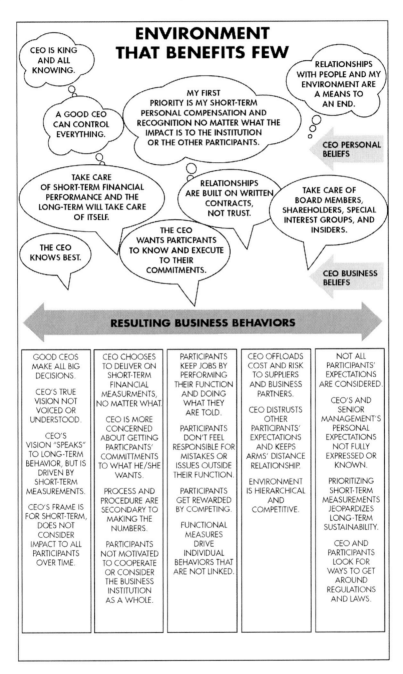

The CEO's personal beliefs are the basis for his business beliefs stated in the second row of Figure 7.1.

The stated vision isn't what he truly believes. His true priorities do not support the long-term sustainability of the business. His primary commitment is to himself and his own measurements and compensation. His priorities may include the expectations of a subset of the participants because he needs them to reach his personal goals but not include the expectations of *all* participants.

The long-term impact of short-term decisions is not taken into consideration. Just as a flick of the wrist can result in the end of a whip traveling at incredible speeds and doing significant damage, a short-term decision for quick profits can cause significant damage to the long-term health of the business.

The CEO's business beliefs produce behavior that demonstrates the focus on short-term P&L performance with resources mainly directed at the next one-to-two year horizon and few resources assigned to the time frame beyond.

The CEO wants to make the P&L and period goals to meet his own, board of directors', investors', or senior management's expectations, even if there is a significant negative impact on the long-term sustainability of the business or to the remaining participants. The CEO may say, "I'm on the team for the long haul," when his unspoken belief is that he's on the team as long as he gets his personal compensation and recognition in the short-term.

When CEOs in publically traded companies make investors' and stockholders' expectations for rising stock price a top priority, they drive functional activities out of alignment, putting stress on the health of the business and the people. The rest of the participants do not get their expectations met while being in an environment that is toxic. The disconnect and the false beliefs that drive these business conditions produce inappropriate levels of stress and compromise the DNA and life expectancy of the company.

In the current environment, true mapping of the interacting relationships of the work and communications systems does not exist.

The Relationship Flows of the desired environment do not exist. The organizational structure limits the frame, with internal functions (engineering, sales, production, etc.) operating like silos. Specific functional measurements drive individual behavior, ignoring the interconnectedness of humans and functions that exists. The CEO believes senior management should make all the decisions and that employees should fall in line and do whatever it takes to execute the business plan and make the forecasted short-term financial results.

The CEO believes that suppliers and business partners are necessary only to deliver the company's products and services. He negotiates strong one-sided contracts that make him feel as if he is in control of those relationships.

Missed period forecasts and goals result in horrendous amounts of detail at non-value-added levels in the company to defend against being blamed. The attitude of "the numbers not being met" causes high levels of stress and fear of failure to the extreme. This environment looks fragmented with participants' beliefs not being openly known. Behavior is unpredictable; it is unsafe to speak openly. When human beings operate from emotions of fear, anger, and dread, they stay stuck. Unless the leader has the trust of participants, decisions will not be made and implemented. The institution will not move forward.

In this current environment, the CEO is not interested in having a dialogue and is not ready to change his personal belief of being in control. He and the managers that he has put in place have been rewarded financially and with other forms of recognition throughout their careers for holding to these beliefs. It may take a business catastrophe or personal trauma to create the opening for them to consider challenging the untruths they have held as true for so long.

The imbalance of a CEO in harmony with some participants' expectations but disconnected with the expectations of other participants—especially employees and customers—causes broken trust between the CEO and the participants. This happens in both privately held and publically traded companies.

Now that we've described the frame of the environment that benefits few—where trust is broken, resources are misdirected, and long-term sustainability is subordinated to short-term expectations of some participants—let's imagine the desired frame where trust achieves long-term sustainability.

The frame of the environment that produces trust: Thoughts ~ Words ~ Behavior = Integrity

When the CEO takes on the new belief and behavior model of trust, he operates with integrity by aligning his personal and business beliefs, thoughts, words, and behavior. He creates and articulates his vision for the long-term sustainability of the business institution (Figure 7.2), which becomes reality as it is shared with and implemented by the participants. This is done in an environment in which participants know and agree to the behavior that is required of them to realize their expectations.

Figure 7.2: Trust is the Basis for Sustainability

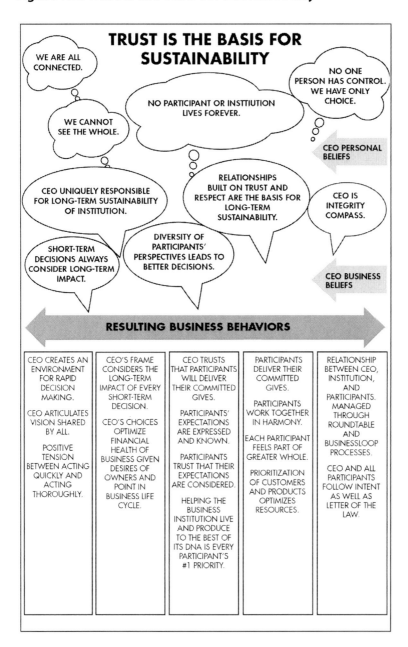

In Figure 7.2, the CEO's personal beliefs are depicted in the clouds across the top of the chart. He believes that the business institution and all of its participants are connected and that none of them will live forever. Knowing that no one, himself included, can ever see all of the connections that make up the whole, he accepts that he can never be in control and seeks tools to make the best choices possible given what can be known.

More than likely, he is not having daily conversations with others about his personal beliefs, no matter how enlightened he may be. However, his personal beliefs are clearly the basis of his expressed business beliefs, which are represented in the second row of Figure 7.2.

The CEO acknowledges his responsibility for the long-term sustainability of the business institution and carries that out by building relationships based on trust and respect with all of the participants. He creates the environment for participants to make effective decisions through their diversity of experiences and by taking into consideration the long-term impact of short-term choices. He *is* the integrity compass of the institution.

In the real world, whether expressed or unexpressed, the CEO's business beliefs drive his behavior, which sets the expected behaviors of all other participants. The lower section of Figure 7.2 categorizes this behavior.

The CEO's frame considers the long-term impact of every short-term decision. The CEO makes choices to optimize the financial health of the business given the desires of its owners and the point in its life cycle. Positive tension exists between acting quickly and acting thoroughly to execute to the P&L and balance-sheet goals.

Participants trust that being who they are and thinking the way they think will be received and considered as long as they continuously manage the business institution's relationships through the RoundTable and BusinessLoop processes. Even if they are not understood, they won't be attacked personally or blocked from speaking. This frees them up to express what they are thinking and feeling intuitively as well as what they "know." This environment contributes to a broader frame for decision making and produces better decisions for the good of the institution and its long-term sustainability.

This does not mean that all participants have their expectations met in the timeframe they would like or even at all. It does mean that all participants trust that their expectations will be considered and weighed along with the expectations of all the other participants in the context of the long-term sustainability of the business institution.

Making short-term decisions that produce a profit but compromise survivability will shorten the sustainability of all companies. When large firms, such as Enron and Lehman Brothers, that are seemingly healthy and reporting profits, fail, it may seem as if the failure came about quickly. In reality, the seeds were sown much earlier, and decisions over time led to their demise.

- What aspects of the environment of the benefits to few are you living with?

- What is the detail in the frame of your BusinessLoop in each of the A, B, C environments in Figure 5.6B?

- What beliefs drive your perception of this framing?

- How do you want to challenge your company?

- Are your personal and business beliefs aligned to lead this challenge? If not, where are they mis-aligned? Does this concern you?

Chapter 8

Changing Your Environment
by Changing Your Focus

"Faith is taking the first step, even when you don't see the whole staircase."

— Martin Luther King, Jr.

The bridge from the current to the desired environment begins with the CEO.

You have completed your self-evaluation by comparing your beliefs and behaviors against those of the environment that benefits few and the environment that rebuilds trust. Reflections and CEO Moments have caused you to think differently about institutional relationships. You are now ready to develop you own pictorial of the environment that supports your vision for your business.

Old beliefs will continue to drive old behavior. Beliefs, yours first and then the business's participants', must change. CEO Exercise 4 will help you solidify your beliefs and begin to move the company you lead toward the desired environment you want to reach. The chart is broken into two parts. The top half is for you to complete. Start by penciling in your own personal beliefs in the clouds. Then fill in your business beliefs just below.

CEO Exercise 4: Your Desired Environment

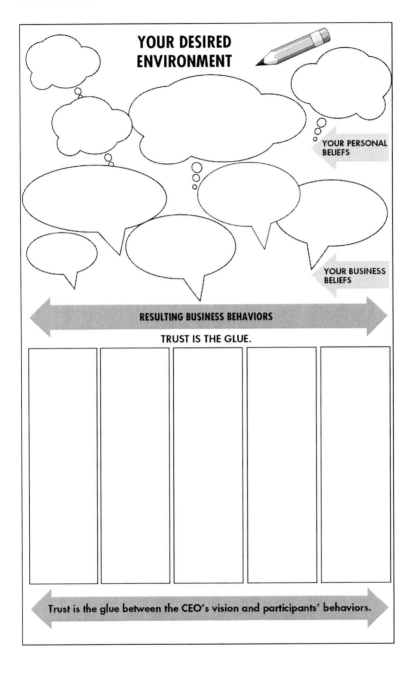

Compare your beliefs with those of the trust environment expressed in Figure 7.2. Are they more similar to the desired beliefs or more like those in the environment that benefits few (Figure 7.1)?

You may be unsure because you haven't thought about leadership in this way before. Perhaps you have a feeling of agreement but are stuck on some of the details. The scope of change that you are facing may be challenging or unsettling to you. Only you can decide to align your beliefs with the beliefs and behaviors of the environment of trust. You must do so before asking others to accept and align their beliefs.

You can't create this environment (any more than you can create any environment) by yourself. You must rely on the institution's participants to deliver on the commitments necessary to implement your new vision. The bottom section of this chart is your starting point for including your participants.

Use this exercise as a tool to introduce others to your new ideas, to reinforce and gain support for the change process, and to address the issues that your management team perceives as they take on the responsibility of implementation. You can use this step as the focus of an offsite RoundTable with your direct reports led by an industrial psychologist and facilitator.

The off-site brings the necessary participants together in your own environment to rebuild trust between you and your participants so that they can begin supporting your vision. Think of trust as the human glue that is necessary to bridge the CEO's vision and the participants' behaviors. I don't have the truth of your environment. I don't have the solutions to your issues and opportunities. But you and your participants do.

Begin to change your environment

I hope you are feeling the potential benefits to yourself and your business, but you may have questions of how to realize those benefits through your participants' implementation. You read the instructions and understand them mentally, now you are ready to apply them and face the challenges from yourself and other participants as you expand the RoundTable and BusinessLoop methodologies to achieve your P&L and balance sheet objectives.

When you go back into your own environment and try to do something unique that others haven't seen you do, you will be challenged. You will challenge yourself. Others, including board members and, if your company is publicly traded, at the very least stock analysts, are going to be challenging you, too.

The "Yeah, Buts" in Chapter 9 prepare the CEO to address the issues that will inevitably bubble up from participants and outsiders as she states her vision for the long-term sustainability of the business institution. Her responses will be built on the beliefs and behaviors of the environment of trust.

CEO REFLECTIONS

- Do you see trust as the basis for achieving sustainability by aligning beliefs?

- Can you articulate the behaviors you desire from yourself and your participants?

- Do your and their beliefs promote those behaviors?

- What must you do in your specific situation to maintain or recreate trust between yourself and your participants to have trust be a true asset on your balance sheet?

Chapter 9

Dialogue with Leadership

"The people who oppose your ideas the most are those who represent the establishment that your ideas will upset."

— Anthony J. D'Angelo, author of *The College Blue Book*

Trust: The CEO's Currency for Success didn't unfold to me in one day. My understanding and acceptance grew as I applied the philosophical concepts of this approach *and* gained practical experience by implementing the RoundTable and BusinessLoop tools.

When I'm consulting with CEOs and others, no matter where they are on the continuum of beliefs, they follow along initially, either because they agree "conceptually" or because they have a problem they need to solve and something in these ideas and tools stimulated them. Inevitably our conversation reaches a point where the person I'm talking with says, "yeah, but." That's when the questions and answers begin surfacing and we can start recognizing the hurdles in applying this model.

In the spirit of dialogue, not debate, the goal of this chapter is to respectfully acknowledge and address the "yeah, buts" that challenge the philosophy of new beliefs, and challenge the pragmatic new behaviors and broader frame of reality resulting from trust.

This question and answer format in a sequence simulates my experience consulting with CEOs. As objections start to surface, either that person is becoming thoughtfully engaged or is looking for a way to end the conversation. Either way, acknowledging or addressing each "yeah, but" is a requisite step in moving toward trust. Even though your situation will be unique, this dialogue will help you anticipate your own "yeah, buts" and the ones that will come from others as you move from your current environment to the desired environment of trust.

Section 1: The challenge of this philosophy

"We've survived previous crises and of leadership; don't you think we'll survive this one, too?"

We can, if we change the way we lead and stop expediting the decline and failure of our business institutions through our individual and collective behavior. History does not bode well for a country or civilization that has been forced to face as many problems both on the economic and social level as we do today. Debt has destroyed the ability of many individuals, business institutions, and communities to survive. Short-term focus dominates at the expense of the long-term. We have become a nation of special interests. This is true in business as well as government and all other institutions.

Broad, deep change is needed for us to resolve long-term issues. Either we believe that broad, deep change is possible and we will get together, roll up our sleeves, and lead through it, or, like others, we'll throw up our hands in despair. Agreement is needed, and it will only come about when we change our beliefs and behaviors. We can't rely on government alone to address the issues we are facing. It is up to us, our nation's business leaders to develop the trust that is needed to change our environment from our current morass to our desired state.

"Yeah, but, I have business problems to solve. Isn't this beliefs and behavior talk too philosophical?"

If you feel that this talk is too philosophical and not pragmatic enough, then the point of the book has passed you by.

Everything comes back to beliefs—especially the CEO's beliefs. If someone would have told me when I was flying over to Europe to meet Herr Braxmeir that *beliefs drive behavior,* I probably would have said, interesting point, but I have a job to do.

My focus was on finding a way to align the business participants' behaviors to meet our P&L and balance sheet goals. When I became aware of language, borders, cultures, I became aware that there are deep seated beliefs behind people's behaviors that determine their perceived frame. The process of understanding and challenging the beliefs behind behaviors will test you to change them, modify them, or at least not just accept them.

You want to change people's behavior, and not just for the short term. You want the change to last when you aren't present to influence their decision-making process. You will use the pragmatic tools of RoundTable and BusinessLoop along with your own financial tools of P&L and balance sheet.

"I might just tell people that they have to act the way I want them to act. If the people who work for me won't change their beliefs, what's wrong with forcing them to change their behavior?"

I can tell that you were trained in hub and spoke as I was. In this new environment, we would like everyone to readily accept the beliefs and behaviors that are behind *Trust: The CEO's Currency for Success.* In reality, that isn't going to happen. We cannot control participants' option to choose. Think about my experience with the Canadian pricing Table.

No CEO is going to fire the current participants and hire new ones just because she is undertaking a new method of leadership. You will first try to work with the participants you have. To an extent, you can require people's behavior to follow the model of this book. The content and envelope tools of the RoundTable, dialogue instead of debate, and RoundTable etiquette all help with this.

Give participants the opportunity to change their behaviors and beliefs but eventually, if a person cannot accept the new beliefs of this way of leading, you have to change them out. The important thing is that without exception the CEO's behavior must always model the new beliefs. If she can choose to behave outside the model, then others can choose that also.

"This concept of choice not control is hard to accept."

Whether you say it or someone else says it, as soon as the word "control" comes into your mind or into the conversation it should be a red flag.

We have seen through world and national events how we are all affected by local as well as around-the-world behavior of others. The CEO and all other participants, no matter where they are in the organization structure and the BusinessLoop, are connected and affected by the behavior produced by others' choices. Human variability is always present, which is the choice to do good or the choice to do bad. If the CEOs of some Wall Street firms really had control in 2008, do you think they would have gotten themselves into the mess they did?

Participants in the business have a choice to stay focused or day dream, to work the full eight-hour day or to spend half of it on the Internet, or to behave ethically or not. Executing a choice might be easy or difficult based on the conditions caused, in large part, by others' choices and behavior, but for sure no one can control another person's choices.

"You say that long-term sustainability is uniquely the responsibility of the CEO. Who's going to argue with that?"

From a philosophical standpoint, probably no one or at least very few. Our problem exists because even the conscientious, well-intended CEOs have not created a large enough frame that encompasses all the participants' expectations and contributions along with their responsibility for the long-term sustainability of the institution. The majority of us must agree to the new relationships between the institution, all of its individual participants and participant groups, and the CEO before this frame, and its resulting influences, can have its positive effect.

The CEO has to have the mental capacity and authority to make decisions to execute his responsibility while balancing the expectations and contributions of all the participants. Other participants may have the desire and the capability, but if they cannot influence the behavior of all who participate in the business institution, they cannot be effective. The CEO is the only individual with this institutional authority and influence.

If the CEO doesn't believe and behave for the long-term sustainability of the institution, it won't matter whether anyone else does or not.

"As CEO, what do I tell all the participants who don't trust anyone in authority?"

At different times in our recent past, there have been disasters (dot-com failure, S&L collapse, Hurricane Katrina), but none of these affected all of us. However, the events of the last years are bringing more and more of us mentally out of the stands and onto the playing field. Most of us have been affected by these events. We have been impacted by others' poor performance and behavior. We all were on the field whether we recognized it or not. We all condoned and allowed for it to go on, as opposed to calling for and demanding the appropriate people to be accountable for their actions and their choices. We need stronger leaders to stand against the temptation and the narrow thinking of the current environment that benefits few. This isn't simple.

All of us have to support somebody in leadership. We can't leave the playing field of society. We are all on it. We aren't allowed to sit in the stands as if we can only complain about how the players are behaving or the decisions of the referees. We are in this together by being connected through our individual behaviors, and we don't have a choice not to be affected.

Gaining trust between any two participants takes the same process, no matter what their level in the organization happens to be. We trust the accountants, the network operator, and the sales manager because they are trained to perform their specialty. A person wouldn't take on the role of accountant or sales person without training and tools.

The CEO is no different. You just don't pick this up. You need to be trained. As important as it is to say, "I hold this broad perspective," you must be trained and have the tools to do it. To earn trust, you must have a perspective gained from holding a broad enough frame to contain all the seemingly disparate parts of the whole. This perspective allows decision making that consider long-term sustainability and the commitments and expectations over time of all the participants.

"Yeah, but, the participants being heard sets the expectation that they will get what they want and we know there are not enough resources for everyone to get their expectations met."

Participants must trust that their desires are being at least considered, and the RoundTable and BusinessLoop methodology offers that.

Some will be able to understand and accept the limits on resources; others won't. But we do need the support of the majority to lead. Companies are limited by their resources. You have to budget and make choices, and that means trade-offs.

At the layers, people see the intensity of their opportunities and issues at 100 percent, but they don't see the intensity of all the opportunities and issues at 100 percent. They have to trust that your frame includes all at 100 percent, and that the rights of all participants are protected and in balance with the institution's. They won't appreciate the leadership having to do the balancing and get the resources when they feel that the institution's resources have been squandered, misused, or siphoned to the benefit to few.

No one's rights, whether individual or group, are entitled to infringe on the rights of others. Mistakes will be made and we will work our way through them. Not by demanding, condemning, and blaming but by voicing and implementing those options and choices for the collective long-term good of the whole.

"Yeah, but, participants are jaded. What is needed in leadership behavior that earns their trust?"

Every short-term action has a long-term effect. If a leader promises to hold the long-term sustainability of the business institution as his or her number-one priority but can't say why a given short-term action is good for the future, then participants won't, and shouldn't, trust and follow. For every action that the CEO is expecting to be done in the short-term, he should be telling the participants the expected or desired impact on the long-term.

It is important that participants know that the future is being considered. By sharing and having considerations stand the light of day, there will be other participants who might step forward and ask, wait a minute, have you considered this? This will offer up more options and buy-in by the participants.

This open process creates a virtual RoundTable resulting in a better outcome. CEOs and leaders contribute by holding to a bigger, broader perspective. If, as CEO, you follow the RoundTable process to set the example of framing the issue and opportunity in the broadest environment possible, you will get others' opinions. Using BusinessLoops to see the issue or opportunity collectively and how its solution impacts other participants, now and over time, tends to make alternatives more clear and produce better decisions. Everyone can appreciate and possibly support these decisions, whether they agree with the specifics or not.

When you have big problems with simple answers, you are not seeing the whole. With a bigger frame and the beliefs of "we can't see the whole" and "we are all connected," you will set different priorities and make different choices to act.

"So how do you create a frame that can hold the immensity of all the relationships and influences and still have it manageable?"

The truth is that we will never see all the influences and connections that exist. It might be impossible to manage all of the pieces, but this is our collective reality. That you asked this question says that you have grasped one of the most important concepts of this book. Don't burden yourself with trying to be perfect.

Get on with it by following the RoundTable process, knowing that with every decision there will be unexpected, unseen, and unintended consequences because everything is connected and no one person or group of people can see it all. Don't strive for perfection. Use the RoundTable and BusinessLoop to make the best, most informed decisions and when something doesn't work, try something else.

The CEO must expand her frame and see the results of her and others behavior on all, not just some, of the participants. Whenever you are evaluating issues and opportunities, take into consideration that all participants are part of the conditions of the environment. Ask the question, "how does this affect all of the participant groups, not just me and/or the Board?" Ask the question group by group, even if you think some participant group is not affected. Don't assume.

"No CEO of a publicly traded company can withstand the pressure of earnings per share quarter by quarter when everybody looks to stock price as the measure of business institutional health."

If we have two CEOs in competing businesses, with different participants, one privately held and one publically held, a big difference between the two is the influence from Wall Street and analysts. What would be the added benefit to the business that has the price of publically traded stock as a measurement versus the one that does not? What is the hierarchy of priorities for each? Are these priorities in the long-term interest and sustainability of the business? Are there gains to all the participants? Does stock price only affect those who are holding the stock when they sell it? Yes. It means that those holding and selling stock do have an interest in the short-term fluctuation of its price. Who else? The institution? No. Stock price as a measurement of the business's success is contrary to the long-term sustainability of the business.

The Board, public or private, that truly believes its number-one responsibility is the long-term sustainability of the institution, will encourage the CEO to spend more of his or her time with customers. The financial success and the longevity of the institution will always translate back to the satisfaction of the customer. Customers are the participant group that is paying the bills and supplying the cash to meet participants' expectations. This is why the business started in the first place, and it is the businesses' lifeblood.

As difficult as it is, a bigger portion of the CEO's time should be spent with the end-users of his company's products and services instead of with Wall Street analysts. Being with customers/users, the CEO will get a true understanding of how the company is addressing the expectations of his customers. Translating these experiences back into the company to make transitions and changes for increased long-term sustainability is a better use of time than catering to Wall Street.

"Isn't it wishful thinking to have all CEOs give up their short-term gains from stock options and salary?"

You have to be creative with the CEO's compensation to make long-term sustainability of the institution your first priority. This isn't about being paid less. It is about being paid for long-term sustainability of the business and overcoming the influences for short-term results. If the CEO and the board of directors truly believe the number-one priority is long-term sustainability of the institution, the CEO's compensation should be reflecting that belief. Once you and your Board accept these beliefs, you will come up with creative ways of doing this for your particular environment. Then, every time the CEO goes into a board meeting, she talks about long-term sustainability the same way as quarterly profits—even more so.

Section 2: Roundtable and BusinessLoop Tools

"Does the RoundTable really have to start with the CEO?"

Yes and the CEO cannot make any exception to the expected behavior.

There might be pockets of RoundTable, but if it isn't driven and modeled by the CEO and the rest of the company's leadership it won't take hold and be sustainable. Through RoundTable and BusinessLoops, participants will understand more fully how they want their leaders to behave, and that they have the responsibility to support the CEO and other leaders if they are carrying out their responsibility in the committed way.

The CEO cannot accept inappropriate behavior at any level. You can't allow anyone to not follow the RoundTable methodology. Otherwise, you will have the RoundTable floating in a sea of rectangular behavior, or you have the rectangular exception confusing participants as a work-around or as an excuse to stay with the old beliefs. Either way, you will never get the desired environment without fully embracing the RoundTable and BusinessLoop methodology in all activities of all participants.

"What if people aren't well-intended?"

You don't know what people are thinking in their clouds, so you don't know if they are well-intended or not. But if you follow the RoundTable process that says every question and comment is worth addressing, if nothing else, you will find out who is well-intended and who is not. In fact, the only way you will get to the true intention is by addressing everyone's comments and concerns, and by giving them the chance to speak, be listened to, and be understood. This does not mean that others will necessarily agree with the expressed point of view.

The CEO isn't dismissive. Approach everything as dialogue, even if someone else approaches it as argument and debate. Until the person proves himself or herself otherwise, the RoundTable process assumes good intentions. Once bad intentions become known, the group is responsible for self-disciplining.

If it can't, the CEO has to supply the discipline to prevent people from circumventing the process. Everyone understands the rigor and the intent of the process that was put in place. The CEO and other leaders must enforce the rules passionately for the long-term good of the whole. If part of the process or rigor is found to be not beneficial, then change the process. Until rules or regulations are changed everyone follows the rules.

"Yeah, but, doesn't this RoundTabling take a long time? There are times when you just have to make the quick decision. Sometimes CEOs just have to step in."

Each time I implemented this approach for the first time in a new environment, various members of my team told me they didn't have time for so much discussion. Let's just do it.

Following RoundTable and BusinessLoop protocols in all daily decision making ingrains the new beliefs of not seeing the whole, we are all connected, and every short-decision has long-term effects. Once we hold the same frame and these beliefs, we also allow for the possibility that something could happen to interrupt our agreed-upon actions.

Just because participants are following the RoundTable and BusinessLoop methodology doesn't preclude having a process to use in an emergency. There will be situations where pressure to make a decision or take an action is so great you do not have the time to convene or reconvene a RoundTable. That's why you do scenario planning up front. This makes a great topic for a Round-Table discussion in quieter times.

Define urgency versus emergency for your environment, thoughtful execution versus just execution, and quick response versus instant reaction. Then communicate that back to the Round-Table and let the participants plan for the various scenarios.

When an unexpected event requires that uninformed decisions be made in the moment without the benefit of the Round-Table, RoundTable participants will be accepting as long as the agreed-upon RoundTable process has been followed. That's part of the trust that the RoundTable builds up. After the urgency subsides, participants who made the emergency decisions inform the affected RoundTable of the situation and what was done.

Remember Bend & Send? It wasn't that Uncle Jerry made a decision in the moment given the conditions he was experiencing. It was the fact that he didn't have the tools of BusinessLoop and RoundTable to communicate back his decision to change the order. If he had, it would have given other business functions the chance to adjust their expectations or possibly influence his. If Uncle Jerry had just shared his decision, Bend & Send might not have been stuck with an unfilled order for pink hangers and cartons of white ones that no one wanted.

A sense of urgency with purposeful direction gives the best chance of positive yield. You want that sense of urgency to execute while being appropriately inclusive. You don't want people justifying "emergency" actions to get around the RoundTable.

We need to believe and support decentralized decision making so that when something unexpected happens at the extremities, action is taken as rapidly as possible. We cannot know when these emergencies will arise, but we do use RoundTable, Business-

Loops, and scenario planning to have an agreed-upon process for response.

Section 3 – Creating the desired environment

"What if by implementing the Roundtable and BusinessLoop, we conclude that the business isn't sustainable?"

Nothing is forever; everything changes. Why would a business institution be any different? It isn't. Everything is temporary if you put a long enough calendar on it. There is no such thing as survivability. At best, it is long-term sustainability

If the business is not sustainable for whatever reason, then you don't put in measurements that suggest that it is. Instead, you communicate to everyone the true condition of the situation and what you propose to do to manage it smaller or even out of existence. You are clear on your priorities and your responsibility to execute given the conditions of the institution's environment. We will stay with current products and services, sell the business, or close the doors. This gets the situation into the light of day with integrity, and the remaining participants can make a decision about whether they choose to stay or go.

This isn't to say that everyone will follow blissfully. The goal is to have transparent and open communications, and then participants can decide whether or not they want to be involved. I believe strongly in this. For participants to be able to choose, they have to know the truth. We are giving our framework and methodology that forges and maintains trust between the participants. If not these, what are yours? Not everyone is willing to follow a model of integrity. We are seeing people's behavior not matching their beliefs and leaving huge problems for the rest of us to solve that are destroying any bond of trust.

"I obey the law, but finding the loopholes is part of the game. If the government can't write a law without a loophole, that's their problem."

Certainly deregulation, the failure to enforce laws, the unintended negative consequences of some regulations, and the unending quest by some participants to circumvent the intent of these laws contributed to our crises. We have too many people looking for loopholes. We all know the intent of laws. If the original intent isn't being achieved or if the law is outdated, then we ought to find a way to change the law.

"Yeah, but, that's just the way the system works. We aren't going to change it. We just need to be smarter than the next guy to succeed within it."

It used to be that our collective behavior demonstrated that we valued integrity and law, but now it appears that we have changed either our values and beliefs or at least our willingness to adhere to them. In too many cases, we have allowed our principles to be high-jacked and our values to be replaced with false beliefs of entitlement and greed. It's a lot of us, in all walks of life, who deliberately chose this slippery slope.

If the system is corrupted, who built the system? Did the current people who are corrupt come from corrupt families, or did they come from families who believed if you don't earn it with integrity, you don't deserve it?

So if it wasn't learned in their family, how did the system sidetrack them? The desire for and ability to influence ethical behavior was missing. They were lured or seduced, and regulation and laws didn't stop the system from staying corrupted. They were role-modeled into the system. You do have to have leadership with integrity. If it isn't the current leadership, then you need the next generation. So how do we get the current generation of leadership to change or get a new generation of changed leadership?

We can influence, even force behavior, but we can't force integrity. That's an inside job. We must move toward our desired environment where integrity is a demanded, integral attribute of leadership and of all participants. Its absence is a big part of the problem and must be a cornerstone of our solutions.

"Sounds like we should redefine Chief Executive Officer as Create Everlasting Order?"

You are making a joke, but that might not be a bad idea. We won't have continual order if we don't try to understand all the influences and connections that exist. Even under revolution, anarchy, and upheaval, there is some vision by the revolutionary leadership of what the steady state of order will look like to them. All the participants might not be in agreement and view the transition as chaos, but there are a few who want an order that gives them the false feeling of control. With the beliefs and behaviors that enable trust, the CEO will create not everlasting order but order that lasts for the institution's life.

CEO REFLECTIONS

After reading this chapter, test your own "yeah, buts." Are you asking questions to understand more of the whole, or are you looking for a reason not to have to consider changing your behavior or beliefs? Just as you are experiencing this "yeah, but" process, so will the other participants in your business, to understand and accept or to deny and stay stuck.

Chapter 10

CEO Moments Morph to Radical Thoughts

In the last ten years or so, my CEO Moments have become more than moments of awareness when the rake hit me in the face. These accumulating CEO Moments along with application and reflection over time have helped generate a new set of personal and business beliefs that resulted in this next level of thinking.

When I implemented the desired environment, I found beliefs and behaviors that mis-directed and detracted from rapid decision making, burdened the organization's P&L with additional cost and steps, kept issues from being addressed, stratified the organization along hierarchical and functional lines, and ultimately broke down trust.

Every business institution, regardless of whether it is public or privately held, is appropriately driven by its P&L and balance sheet. A business cannot be long-term sustainable without being able to fund short-term operations. However, the sustained overemphasis on short-term profits, as evidenced by prevalent methods of CEO compensation and using stock price as a performance measurement, has eaten away at the long-term sustainability of company after company.

Changing beliefs on CEO compensation and measurement

What better way to test your own core beliefs, business beliefs, and business behavior than to assess how you feel about your own compensation. What you want to be compensated for is the strongest indicator of what you truly believe your responsibility really is. Put your mark on the continuum of beliefs regarding compensation and stock price in CEO Exercise 5.

CEO Exercise 5: Radical Thoughts on Compensation and Stock Price

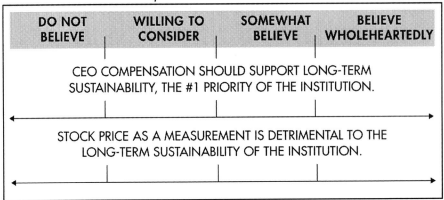

DO NOT BELIEVE	WILLING TO CONSIDER	SOMEWHAT BELIEVE	BELIEVE WHOLEHEARTEDLY

CEO COMPENSATION SHOULD SUPPORT LONG-TERM SUSTAINABILITY, THE #1 PRIORITY OF THE INSTITUTION.

STOCK PRICE AS A MEASUREMENT IS DETRIMENTAL TO THE LONG-TERM SUSTAINABILITY OF THE INSTITUTION.

Radical Thought #1: CEO compensation systematically misdirects CEOs.

When CEOs, their boards of directors, and a company's senior leadership are compensated with stock options—especially when this is the major portion of their compensation—it shouldn't be any surprise that they are highly motivated to deliver higher short-term profits in hopes of driving up the share price. When a CEO's compensation is driven by stock price, how will his short-term actions to drive that price up impact the long-term sustainability of the company?

The problem created, as most CEOs understand only too well, is that the constant pressure on creating short-term earnings per share all too often comes at the expense of the future growth, and even the long-term sustainability, of the company. This is the root of the CEO's dilemma.

RADICAL THOUGHT #1
We have systematically misdirected our nation's CEOs through their compensation.

RADICAL THOUGHTS

I firmly believe that most CEOs did not take the job of CEO *just* to make more and more money or to receive more and more recognition or perks. There is a higher good to be achieved for the benefit of the institution and all of its participants—the long-term sustainability of the institution done with integrity. Don't get me wrong. This is not a statement about the amount of compensation a CEO receives. I believe CEOs should be richly compensated for achieving a vision that leads a company to long-term sustainability. I take issue with tying compensation to short-term results when the CEO's responsibility is to execute a vision that spans years.

"It is difficult to get a man to understand something when his salary depends upon him not understanding it."

— Upton Sinclair, author of *The Jungle*

Suppose for a moment that CEO compensation supported instead of conflicted with CEO responsibility for the long-term sustainability of the institution. Would more CEOs be willing to view the institution as a separate entity and lead with a broader frame that allows for the possibility of all the influences of all the participants that exist in the real environment? Would CEOs be more able to acknowledge that we are all connected, that no one can see the whole, that we have choice not control, and that we cannot lead without being trusted? Would more participants be willing to trust that their expectations were being considered in a larger frame and be less focused on being treated as a special interest and receiving their desires in the short-term?

I believe the answer to these questions is yes, yes, yes.

Why would any well-intended participants in the company want the CEO's number-one priority to be anything other than long-term sustainability? The answer is they wouldn't.

And if the participants in the company wouldn't want this kind of measurement for their leadership, then who would want the CEO to be measured and compensated on stock price, making quarterly goals her number-one priority?

The answer is stock analysts, brokers, and shareholders of the company's publically traded stock. The problem with this approach is that these entities are not participants in the company. They deliver no value to the business institution in return for their expectations being met. The stock price of publically traded companies is often touted as a measure of the company's success, when in reality, the company's success will be determined by the delivered commitments of the company's participants—not the holders or traders of its stock.

Radical Thought #2: Stock price is not a measure of company success.

Assuming the stock is not a new issue, there is no financial value to the business institution when an individual or institutional investor purchases or sells existing shares of stock or when the price of the stock goes up or down. Only the person or institution holding and selling the stock in that time frame has the potential for benefit. If there is no financial value to the business institution, chasing stock price is disconnected from the health of the business and from good decision making.

"On average U.S. corporations now lose half their customers in five years, half their employees in four, and half their investors in less than one."

— Frederick F. Reichheld, author of *The Loyalty Effect*

To consider short-cycle stockholders or stock analysts as participants, we must ask, what are they contributing to the business institution in order to get some or all of their expectations met? If they do not give something that contributes to the long-term sustainability of the institution, then they are not truly participants. This means they do not deserve an expectation to be met. They should not be of influence.

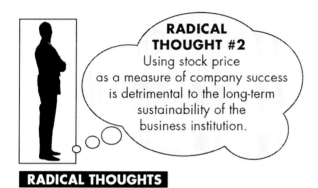

RADICAL THOUGHT #2
Using stock price as a measure of company success is detrimental to the long-term sustainability of the business institution.

RADICAL THOUGHTS

CEOs and other leaders have fallen into the trap of either mis-assigning the analysts' true influence on the sustainability of the business institution or, as holders of options and/or stock themselves, have used stock price and analysts' opinions as justification for actions that support their own personal gain. They chase stock price as if it is beneficial to the sustainability of the institution, which it is not.

Betting on the stock price to rise or fall is like betting on a football game. The coach doesn't tell the players to do something differently based on how the people in the stands are betting. It should be the same with the CEO. Making the right decision for the long-term sustainability of the company and having the stock price go up or down are independent events.

There is no single area in this material where I have received more pushback from CEOs and business-people than on the subject of the appropriateness of stock price as a measure of success or the influence it should have on CEO decision making. If my experience is representative, business leaders and Wall Street do not want to give up on stock price as a measure for business performance because of its direct tie to their personal compensation.

But the more I consider and discuss this topic, the more certain I have become. When the current price of the stock is the measure of company and/or CEO performance, there is a crippling effect on the ability of the business institution to be long-term sustainable. When CEOs demonstrate that their motivation is their own personal monetary gain, this ravishes participants' trust and erodes companies' resources.

If not stock price, then what?

Unless we find ways to motivate CEOs and other leaders as strongly for long-term sustainability of the business institutions they lead as options and stock price currently do for their short-term performance, our business institutions will continue to fail ahead of their DNA. Trust between CEOs and participants will further disintegrate. The participants we are relying on to carry out the CEO's vision will become more disillusioned, frustrated, and angry.

It isn't just replacing dollars for short-term performance with dollars for long-term performance. As we have seen, compensation also has to satisfy right brain attributes of inclusiveness, connected to the whole, and contributing to a business institution that survives beyond the relative short-term time frame of our own participation.

It would be Pollyannaish to think it will be simple to find different ways of paying our leadership for performing their responsibility for long-term sustainability—ways that are based on delivering on the expectations of all participants, not just some.

It will not be easy to retrain our Pavlovian response to stock and stock options in compensation. But options have not always been a tool of compensation. We can change our diet if we choose to. Otherwise, famine will cause us to go on a low calorie diet by default.

Changing beliefs challenges disruptive and unnecessary activities

Internally, as RoundTables and BusinessLoops take hold, whistle-blowing, more regulations, class action suits, executive summaries, and the type of participant that I call Side Door Ralph are not needed and in fact are destructive.

More radical thinking can eliminate these five activities and clear the way for business beliefs based on trust to bring about the desired business behaviors.

Radical Thought #3: We do not need whistle-blowers.

In the current environment, participants will tend to support a flawed system for a time even if they don't get their desired expectations met. Participants don't feel empowered to solve the problems they see. Even when the system gets corrupted, participants in the levels and layers may live with the problem, because in a frame limited by organizational hierarchy, they lack the authority to act.

When the situation gets so bad that a "whistle-blower" has the nerve to bring it up, the usual way to get attention is to go outside the organizational structure. Assuming that whistle-blowers are conscientious people wanting to do the right thing for the organization, if they cannot trust their organizational structure and hierarchical authority flow to resolve the issue, they have little choice but to go outside to get attention and force action.

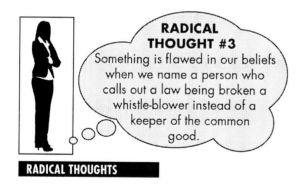

RADICAL THOUGHT #3
Something is flawed in our beliefs when we name a person who calls out a law being broken a whistle-blower instead of a keeper of the common good.

RADICAL THOUGHTS

When we use the term whistle-blower, we aren't including or considering these participants in the frame of the business institution. We are by definition, forcing them to operate outside the frame when they are actually inside.

We don't need whistle-blowers; we need empowered participants at any level of the organization with the support of management and the tools to act. Replace the talk of whistle-blowing with a process that elevates all issues that could be destructive to a participant or the business institution. This is something that all well-intended participants can support. The RoundTable respects that even though an issue isn't a participant's direct responsibility, if that participant sees something that feels out of line, he is encouraged to say, *"I see this happening, and I don't understand why."*

In the desired frame, each participant at any level has the responsibility, resources, and authority to participate in changing the way things are being done for the good of the institution and, therefore, for the good of all the participants. The person having whistle-blower feelings would bring together the affected parties with the authority flowing through the process of the RoundTable methodology to either resolve the problem or elevate it to any other appropriate level in the organizational structure if the solution requires it.

In dealing with issues, either there will be training to address the behavior or there is a very real integrity or ethics issue that the CEO and other leaders must address.

Take the Canadian pricing example in Chapter 6. It didn't take a whistle-blower to alert the CEO to the renegade pricing. The participants who were affected raised the issue at a reconvened RoundTable and it was addressed.

In the desired environment, the whistle-blower is no longer the whistle-blower but an internal protector of participants.

Radical Thought #4: We do not need a lot of new laws.

We want government to set the regulations that deter management and individual behaviors that can negatively affect other institutions and their participants. Laws and regulations are there to weed out those who behave without integrity. There has to be a way to force accountability and implement a remedy in the short-term when processes get compromised by an individual's bad behavior.

But government regulations that were supposed to protect us from the effects of poor behavior have not. Laws and regulations do not replace or substitute for a CEO's integrity and broad frame for visioning. Too many people are looking at government to control behaviors instead of holding the leadership of our institutions accountable.

We want our leaders to act, not out of fear for their jobs but with a sense of what is best for the common good. And when they don't, CEOs should hold each other accountable and be the first to say what behaviors warrant reprimand or punishment.

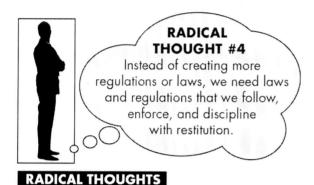

RADICAL THOUGHT #4
Instead of creating more regulations or laws, we need laws and regulations that we follow, enforce, and discipline with restitution.

RADICAL THOUGHTS

We need to administer to the laws and regulations on the books, get rid of the outdated or ineffective ones, and plug the loopholes.

"This country has come to feel the same when Congress is in session as when the baby gets hold of a hammer."

— Will Rogers, author and philosopher

Washington and Wall Street can wrestle with reforms and new regulations to control business behavior. They can debate the behavior forever, but until the beliefs behind those behaviors are out in the open, more laws aren't going to change things. Laws can't force leaders to examine beliefs that disregard—or fail to regard—*all* of the participants' contributions and desires for now and into the future.

Punishing the two villagers who left the gates open for the tigers doesn't make the village society better. But the threat of punishment can possibly deter the next two villagers from future destructive behavior.

Whatever laws and regulations we agree to, we must be willing to uphold them and discipline those who break them. If we aren't willing to require compliance, punish offenders, and gain restitution for those who are damaged or suffer losses, then the laws and regulations shouldn't be in place.

Radical Thought #5: We do not need class action lawsuits.

Class action lawsuits damage the institution. The people who behaved inappropriately and benefited financially may get a hand slap instead of being punished and making full restitution. Most of the participants get hurt, and the life of the institution shortens or ends.

When a participant or group of participants in the business institution makes a bad choice, either by mistake or through a lapse in ethics or integrity, the goal should be to correct the participants' behavior and gain appropriate restitution, not to damage and penalize the institution—thus injuring more people inside and outside the business.

It isn't institutional behavior that broke the law but the behavior of specific people inside institutions. By hurting the institution, class action suits punish *all* the participants in the business institution, whether or not they offended or broke the law. Often the offending participants are the least affected at all. If you hit me, and my way of getting back at you is by hitting your dog, you might feel bad for your dog, but your dog is the one who feels the pain.

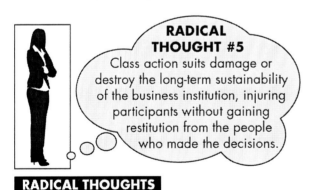

RADICAL THOUGHT #5
Class action suits damage or destroy the long-term sustainability of the business institution, injuring participants without gaining restitution from the people who made the decisions.

RADICAL THOUGHTS

When we punish the business institution and not the participants who broke the law or regulation, we are defeating the long-term sustainability of the business institution.

An autopsy of who created the problem and how, not a class action suit, is required. If greed, corruption, and self-motivated behavior by CEOs and participants have caused the offense, this behavior must be changed through disciplined regulation of and restitution from those participants, not the entire business institution.

Radical Thought #6: We do not use executive summaries to make decisions.

Executive summaries indicate that the CEO or other senior level participants, no matter what their words may be, are withholding authority and not trusting the individual living with the issue to make decisions.

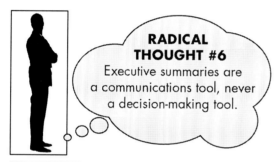

RADICAL THOUGHT #6
Executive summaries are a communications tool, never a decision-making tool.

RADICAL THOUGHTS

The participants living with the business issue have details that an executive summary does not cover. The participant writing the executive summary uses his left brain to distill the detail he lives with to explain or justify decisions and outcomes to upper levels of the organization. The executive summary loses the right brain feeling that so benefits decision making at the point of contact. Important connections and truths are lost.

RoundTable and BusinessLoop processes create the most effective decision making at the appropriate levels of the organization. As upper levels release the authority and resources to the relationship flow, they no longer ask for executive summaries to see if participants are doing their job. The CEO might ask for detail from a participant as input to developing a strategy or to show genuine interest in a participant's contributions and work, but executive summaries are no longer desired or necessary for decision making or protection.

In the new framing of decision making from Relationship Flow instead of organizational levels, the CEO is not indifferent to the decisions that participants make but is often indifferent to the steps of implementation, recognizing that something unforeseen might disrupt the implementation steps that were first agreed upon.

In the desired environment, the executive summary becomes a communications tool. It becomes a summary of the options and recommendations for solving issues by the people who are living with those issues and understand them best. The CEO should refuse to get into the details and not make, but support, the decision once the BusinessLoop and Roundtable processes are followed.

Radical Thought #7: We do not need Side Door Ralphs.

There are a lot of underground ways that things get done in a company, especially a company that has existed for a while. Some work-arounds may be truly more efficient because the formal process is flawed, while other work-arounds are just a power play.

We all know Ralph. He's the guy who, whether well intended or not, always knows how to go around any of the three systems—organization structure, work systems, and communications systems—to get something done. If you really want to know how to get something done, you go to Ralph. He knows how to work around the formal stated system through the side door. He's the one who says, "Don't follow that procedure; it really doesn't work. Here's what you want to do instead."

Maybe it's because Ralph recognizes that internal impediments slow down a company's growth, or maybe he has figured out how to stockpile information as a way to gain stature or control. Regardless of his motivation—whether he's a fast-path, a work-around, or subversive—it is not in the best interest of any company to have the Ralphs of this world operate long-term. And in the larger framing of trust, Ralph becomes unnecessary.

But don't stop Ralph too quickly; he is shining the light on an organizational deficiency—an aspect of the business that management may have thought was working fine but isn't. Instead, bring Ralph to a RoundTable that his work-around affects. It doesn't matter where he reports, his level in the organization, or even what his job is. If Ralph is an influence, the business flow needs Ralph at the specific RoundTable to gain his perspective and see more clearly the issue and options.

RADICAL THOUGHT #7
Side Door Ralph is a beacon for a process that needs changing.

RADICAL THOUGHTS

Bringing Ralph to the RoundTable shows the organization that when there is a better procedure, the agreed-upon RoundTable process is inclusive enough to include it to decide on its merits and costs. It also demonstrates to the organization that side-dooring has no place in the new framing. It is another version of the false belief that one person knows all.

No matter how well intended, Ralph absent a RoundTable is not a good thing. Ralph is actually overriding and undercutting the right brain decision making of the layers. It could be that he's taken on what management really wants—to get the job done no matter what while we look the other way. If you have implemented the RoundTable methodology and still have a Ralph, you have a problem. To eliminate Ralph's negative influence, include his knowledge in the issue through the RoundTable that he is already participating in through the side door.

Carrying forward rebuilding trust

Eliminating executive summaries, whistle-blowers, the call for or expectation of more regulations, class action suits, and Side Door Ralph paves the way for business beliefs to flow to desired business behaviors. There is the left brain linear network of the BusinessLoop with the right brain relationship flow created by the RoundTable process that keeps all the participants connected.

Success isn't having an understanding of issues, problems, and possible solutions. It is having the courage and conviction to make a choice that isn't appreciated by everyone but that is accepted and implemented because the decision-maker and his process are trusted.

Conclusion

The goal of a business institution is sustainability based on its DNA, achieved by taking into account the gives and gets of all of its participants, not just a few.

The thinking required for sustainability is not tied to finding a one-time or even a sometime solution. The mindset, methodology, and continuous processes must be perpetually directed at thinking beyond current products, services, and short-term measurements. The sitting CEO is keeping guard for future generations. As the current custodian, he constantly adjusts to reality as it unfolds, not seeking perfection in daily activities.

CEOs must make current decisions with imperfect data and be responsible for the impacts on all participants in the institution for now and for the future. The fastest and surest path is for CEOs, presidents, and business owners to embrace the belief that the integrity-based leadership philosophy of holistic thinking, diversity of thought, and building trust in relationships is at the core of building sustainable businesses. This focus must be part of the daily culture and operating environment of the institution as modeled by its CEO and leadership.

If you've come this far, you accept that to stop our collective boat from sinking, we must change current behaviors and the beliefs that are driving them. In the preceding chapters, you started developing your plan to bring your participants together to right the boat. The CEO's currency to make and implement decisions in the short-term that lead to long-term sustainability is trust.

TRUST:
The CEO's Currency for Success

The ASSET
that doesn't show on the balance sheet